# Hockey Goaltending

Eli Wilson

Brian van Vliet

**HUMAN KINETICS**

**Library of Congress Cataloging-in-Publication Data**

Names: Wilson, Eli, author. | van Vliet, Brian, author.
Title: Hockey goaltending / Eli Wilson, Brian van Vliet.
Description: Champaign, IL : Human Kinetics, 2018.
Identifiers: LCCN 2017024203 (print) | LCCN 2017033290 (ebook) | ISBN
 9781492559221 (ebook) | ISBN 9781492533801 (print)
Subjects: LCSH: Hockey--Goalkeeping. | Hockey goalkeepers--Training of.
Classification: LCC GV848.76 (ebook) | LCC GV848.76 .W55 2018 (print) | DDC
 796.356--dc23
LC record available at https://lccn.loc.gov/2017024203

ISBN: 978-1-4925-3380-1 (print)

The web addresses cited in this text were current as of May 2017, unless otherwise noted.

**Acquisitions Editor:** Diana Vincer; **Developmental Editor:** Laura Pulliam; **Managing Editors:** Stephanie M. Ebersohl and Ann C. Gindes; **Copyeditor:** Erin Cler; **Permissions Manager:** Martha Gullo; **Graphic Designer:** Whitney Milburn; **Cover Designer:** Keri Evans; **Photograph (cover):** Jeanine Leech/Icon Sportswire; **Photographs (interior):** © Human Kinetics, except figures 1.1-1.5 and 1.6b, © Sport Maska Inc., and figures 1.6a, 1.9, and 1.10a-b, © Chris Gibbs; **Senior Art Manager:** Kelly Hendren; **Illustrations:** © Human Kinetics, unless otherwise noted; **Photo Production Manager:** Jason Allen; **Printer:** Versa Press

Human Kinetics book are available at special discounts for bulk purchase. Special editions or book excerpts can also be created to specification. For details, contact the Special Sales Manager at Human Kinetics.

Printed in the United States of America     10 9 8 7 6 5 4 3 2 1

The paper in this book is certified under a sustainable forestry program.

**Human Kinetics**
P.O. Box 5076
Champaign, IL 61825-5076
Website: www.HumanKinetics.com

In the United States, e-mail info@hkusa.com or call 800-747-4457.

In Canada, e-mail info@hkcanada.com.

In Europe, e-mail hk@hkeurope.com.

For information about Human Kinetics' coverage in other areas of the world, please visit our website: www.HumanKinetics.com

E6846

To my mom, Wendy, who taught me to always keep a positive attitude and be grateful to the people who have impacted my life in a positive way.

—Eli


To my wife, Anna Marie, who supported me unconditionally, and my four kids, Monet, Steven, Melanie, and Tyler, who provided me with constant encouragement throughout this journey.

—Brian

# Contents

Drill Finder     vi         Acknowledgments    xi

Foreword       ix         Introduction       xiii

**Chapter 1**  **Selecting and Fitting Gear** . . . . . . . . . . . . . . . . . . . **1**

Goalie Pads .................................................................. 2

Catch Glove ................................................................. 5

Blocker ........................................................................ 7

Chest Protector ........................................................... 8

Pants ........................................................................... 10

Mask ............................................................................ 10

Skates .......................................................................... 12

Stick ............................................................................. 13

**Chapter 2**  **Stance and Movement** . . . . . . . . . . . . . . . . . . . . . **15**

Stance .......................................................................... 16

Movement .................................................................... 25

Skating and Movement Techniques ........................... 28

Stance and Movement Drills ....................................... 31

**Chapter 3**  **Save Execution** . . . . . . . . . . . . . . . . . . . . . . . . . . . **37**

Fundamentals of Making a Save .............................. 37

The Butterfly ............................................................. 38

Types of Save Executions ........................................ 44

Save-Execution Drills ............................................... 52

**Chapter 4**  **Postsave Recovery** . . . . . . . . . . . . . . . . . . . . . . . . **63**

Postsave Recovery Skills ........................................ 63

Corralling and Covering Rebounds .......................... 76

Postsave Recovery Drills ......................................... 78

**Chapter 5  Puck Handling** . . . . . . . . . . . . . . . . . . . . . **91**

Characteristics of an Effective Puck-Handling
Goaltender . . . . . . . . . . . . . . . . . . . . . . . . . . . . . . . . . . . . . . . . . . . .92
Effective Puck-Handling Skills . . . . . . . . . . . . . . . . . . . . . . . . . . .94
Leaving and Returning to the Net . . . . . . . . . . . . . . . . . . . . . 106
Puck-Handling Drills . . . . . . . . . . . . . . . . . . . . . . . . . . . . . . . . . . . 108

**Chapter 6  Tactics** . . . . . . . . . . . . . . . . . . . . . . . . . . . . . . . **115**

Breakaways . . . . . . . . . . . . . . . . . . . . . . . . . . . . . . . . . . . . . . . . . . . 116
Dekes . . . . . . . . . . . . . . . . . . . . . . . . . . . . . . . . . . . . . . . . . . . . . . . . . 119
Power Play . . . . . . . . . . . . . . . . . . . . . . . . . . . . . . . . . . . . . . . . . . . . 121
Screens . . . . . . . . . . . . . . . . . . . . . . . . . . . . . . . . . . . . . . . . . . . . . . . 123
Tip Shots and Deflections . . . . . . . . . . . . . . . . . . . . . . . . . . . . . 124
Scrambles . . . . . . . . . . . . . . . . . . . . . . . . . . . . . . . . . . . . . . . . . . . . . 124
Plays Off the Rush . . . . . . . . . . . . . . . . . . . . . . . . . . . . . . . . . . . . . 125
Tactic Drills . . . . . . . . . . . . . . . . . . . . . . . . . . . . . . . . . . . . . . . . . . . 127

**Chapter 7  Off-Ice Training** . . . . . . . . . . . . . . . . . . . . . **137**

Flexibility and Mobility Training . . . . . . . . . . . . . . . . . . . . . . . 139
Strength Training . . . . . . . . . . . . . . . . . . . . . . . . . . . . . . . . . . . . . . 164
Speed, Power, and Agility Training . . . . . . . . . . . . . . . . . . . . 179
Stamina Training . . . . . . . . . . . . . . . . . . . . . . . . . . . . . . . . . . . . . . 191
Creating Weekly Training Schedules . . . . . . . . . . . . . . . . . . . 197

**Chapter 8  The Mental Game** . . . . . . . . . . . . . . . . . . . . **199**

The Importance of Mindset . . . . . . . . . . . . . . . . . . . . . . . . . . . .200
Mindset Techniques . . . . . . . . . . . . . . . . . . . . . . . . . . . . . . . . . . . 201
Mind Mapping . . . . . . . . . . . . . . . . . . . . . . . . . . . . . . . . . . . . . . . .209
Goaltender Mindset Drills . . . . . . . . . . . . . . . . . . . . . . . . . . . . . . 211

**Chapter 9  Mentoring the Complete Goaltender** . . . . . . . . **215**

The Goalie Coach . . . . . . . . . . . . . . . . . . . . . . . . . . . . . . . . . . . . . 216
The Head Coach . . . . . . . . . . . . . . . . . . . . . . . . . . . . . . . . . . . . . . 222
The Goaltender . . . . . . . . . . . . . . . . . . . . . . . . . . . . . . . . . . . . . . . 225
The Backup Goaltender . . . . . . . . . . . . . . . . . . . . . . . . . . . . . . . 228

About the Authors          230

# Drill Finder

## Chapter 2: Stance and Movement

Post and Out Drill ...................................................................... 32
Three-Stop Box Drill ................................................................ 33
Two-Stop Box Drill ................................................................... 34
Two-Stop Box With Butterfly Drill ............................................. 35
Post and Out With Butterfly Drill .............................................. 36

## Chapter 3: Save Execution

Moving-Glove Drill .................................................................. 53
Hold-Glove Save ..................................................................... 54
Mirror Save ............................................................................. 55
Post and Out for Shot Drill ....................................................... 56
Side-to-Side Shots Drill ........................................................... 57
Single-Shot Patience Drill ........................................................ 58
Far-Side Stick Save With Second Shot Drill .............................. 59
Double Pass, Double Shot Drill ................................................ 60
Double Lateral Pass and Shot Drill ........................................... 62

## Chapter 4: Postsave Recovery

Reverse Rebound Drill ............................................................. 79
Down and Up Shot Drill ........................................................... 80
Down and Up With a Second Shot ........................................... 82
Up, Across, and Back With a Second Shot ............................... 84
Inside-Edge Push Into Far Post With Lead-Leg Recovery .............. 85
Down and Up, Behind the Net With Breakaway ........................... 87
Post and Out Butterfly With Inside-Edge Push ........................... 89
Up, Across, and Back; Short-Side Shot; and Rebound ................... 90

## Chapter 5: Puck Handling

Forehand and Backhand Pass Drill .......................................... 109
Three-Way Pass Drill .............................................................. 110
Skating Patterns ..................................................................... 111
Dump-In Drill .......................................................................... 112
Clearing the Zone ................................................................... 113
Rims With Options .................................................................. 114

## Chapter 6: Tactics

Short Breakaway .................................................................... 129

Three-Puck Breakaway Drill ................................................ 130

Double Screen ...................................................................... 132

Shot Pass Drill ..................................................................... 133

Pass-In-Front Scramble ...................................................... 134

Pass-In-Front Scramble With Screen .................................. 135

## Chapter 7: Off-Ice Training

Ball on Hip Flexor ............................................................... 145

Ball on Glutes ...................................................................... 146

Ball on Adductor ................................................................. 147

Ball on Foot ......................................................................... 148

Half-Kneeling Groin Stretch With Rock Back ..................... 149

Hip Flexor Stretch With Foot on Wall ................................ 150

Lat Stretch With Hands on Foam Roll ................................ 151

Active Dorsiflexion .............................................................. 152

Figure-Four Stretch ............................................................. 153

Elevated Hamstring Stretch With Active Rotation .............. 154

Quadruped Rock Back With T-Spine Rotation .................... 155

Butterfly Flow ...................................................................... 156

Walking Quad Stretch ......................................................... 157

Walking Knee Hug ............................................................... 158

Hip Shift Down and Back .................................................... 159

Inverted Reach .................................................................... 160

Sumo Squat to Pop ............................................................. 161

Lateral Shuffle to Deceleration .......................................... 162

Wall Juggle With Hip Shift .................................................. 163

Sumo Squat ........................................................................ 167

Tall Kneeling Bungee Press ................................................ 168

Half-Groin Oblique Row ..................................................... 169

Half-Groin Cable Lift ........................................................... 170

Knee Recovery Lateral Hop ................................................ 171

Lateral Lunge Balance ........................................................ 172

Half-Kneeling Bungee Pec Fly ............................................ 173

Push-Up and Reach ............................................................ 174

Reverse Crease Bungee Push ............................................. 175

Squat Jump and Hold .......................................................... 176

Contra Dumbbell Row ......................................................... 177

Three-Way Medicine Ball Squeeze ..................................... 178

### *Chapter 7: Off-Ice Training* (continued)

Lateral Hop and Stick ........................................................................ 182

Quadruped Hip Circles ...................................................................... 183

V Drill................................................................................................ 184

Knee Recovery Lateral Hop and Shuffle .......................................... 185

Wide Out .......................................................................................... 186

Kneeling Shimmy .............................................................................. 187

Pigeon Flow ...................................................................................... 188

Quick Step and Lateral Hop .............................................................. 189

Quick Lateral Shuffle to Knee Down ................................................ 190

High-Knees Jump Rope ..................................................................... 193

Alternate-Knee Recovery .................................................................. 194

Side Plank and Rotate ....................................................................... 195

Shuttle Run ....................................................................................... 196

### *Chapter 8: The Mental Game*

Word Count Drill ............................................................................... 212

Focus Control Drill............................................................................. 212

Positive Success Drill ........................................................................ 213

Self-Affirmation Drill......................................................................... 213

Save Drill ........................................................................................... 213

Save Visualization and Focus Reset Drill 1 ...................................... 214

Save Visualization and Focus Reset Drill 2 ...................................... 214

# Foreword

It was a beautiful September afternoon around 3 o'clock in the afternoon when I started to get ready to leave for my first ever hockey practice at Sturgeon Arena in Edmonton. It was 1973. I was 12 years old and extremely nervous and excited at the same time. Not only was this my first practice, but it was the first time playing goalie.

That decision to try out for the Elmwood community peewee team changed my life forever. I certainly didn't know it at the time, but ultimately my love of the sport—and in particular the challenge of stopping pucks—would guide me down a path that I never envisioned.

I'm sure you, too, can vividly remember your first practice. Maybe you even recall the first save you ever made. There's just something so unique about being a goalie. It's a position where it's almost virtually impossible to get better without being taught all the nuances surrounding the position.

I met Eli Wilson a number of years ago when he was still the goalie coach for the Medicine Hat Tigers, working alongside Willie Desjardins. Willie told me what a great goalie coach Eli is because of his passion about the position. I quickly noticed that as well. Plus, he has an inquisitive mind. He's always trying to learn something new. Both are great qualities when you're talking about a position that was rapidly changing and progressing since the 1980s; no position in any sport has gone through such a dramatic overhaul.

This created an opportunity for Eli to study and teach the position to goalies of all levels and ages. I would occasionally drop by his training center in Calgary and watch him work with young goalies, because I needed to learn the new techniques being taught. I admired his passion and patience, because the position itself is demanding—both physically and mentally.

When I describe the feeling of trying to stop a puck in game conditions, I use the word *intoxicating*. There is not a more powerful feeling than when you're aware that your play can singlehandedly win or lose the game for your team. There is nothing more exhilarating than when you make that key save late in the game to preserve a win and nothing more crushing than when you don't.

But to make that timely save, you need a technique that you can trust under the most stressful times in a game.

That's why I love this book, *Hockey Goaltending*.

Eli has thought about every aspect of goaltending. Nothing is left out, and yet he makes it simple to understand. Every chapter reminds me of all the steps I went through to perform at the highest level in the world.

He talks about the key elements, including balance, stance, and skating. I really enjoyed the off-ice advice given in the book too. Mobility training is crucial for a healthy body and mind. Mental strength is imperative for success and for getting through difficult times, because there will be plenty of those.

Let's go back to 1973. I wanted to learn as much about playing goal as humanly possible. I watched every game broadcast on hockey night in Canada, studying my heroes, and I tried to emulate them my next time on the ice. I researched and studied to develop the proper techniques and tactics. As the sport continues to change and get faster, and players become stronger and more powerful, you too need to research and study the evolution of technical skills and strategy to stop any shot that comes your way. Eli Wilson will get you there with this game-changing resource and develop your ability to be the best goaltender you can be.

—Kelly Hrudey, Former NHL goaltender
and current Hockey Night in Canada broadcaster

# Acknowledgments

I would like to thank numerous people for making this goaltending book possible, beginning with my family and hometown of Maple Ridge, British Columbia, where I got my start in goaltending. All the places that I traveled to and worked in because of the game hold a special place in my heart, most notably, Medicine Hat and Calgary, Alberta; Ottawa, Ontario; Syracuse, New York; and South Korea. Every place I have gone to and all the people I have met are the experiences that I have used to enhance my craft. To move forward in any sport, you need a lot of support around you, and I've been fortunate to have just that. My closest friends are from the game of hockey. I would like to thank all the student goaltenders I have worked with over the years. The fuel that keeps me going is what I do on the ice. I thoroughly enjoy watching as my students pursue their dreams and goals. Many of my goaltenders have had great success outside of the game of hockey. I have had students who became doctors, lawyers, dentists, business owners, coaches, politicians, and, of course, NHL goaltenders. Such results provide me with more reward than anything I have personally accomplished in this game.

I would like to thank Maria Mountain for all her work in ensuring that the off-ice photo shoot went smoothly; Shane Pizzey of Aspire Health and Performance, for generously allowing us the use of his gym; Brett Aynsley and family, for providing the beautiful rink in Kelowna for the on-ice portion of the photo shoot; Tyler van Vliet, Liam McOnie, and Kristen Olychuck, for their excellent work as models for our photo shoot; and Chris Colgan, for his amazing photography.

Finally, I would like to thank my coauthor, Brian van Vliet. We spent the better part of a year talking about goaltending and working tirelessly on this project. The time spent with Brian putting this book together has been one of the most fun and rewarding experiences I have had in the game of hockey.

—Eli

When the opportunity arose for me to write this book with Eli Wilson, to say I jumped at it would be an understatement. It takes the cooperation of so many people to make a project of this nature come to fruition. I especially want to thank my father, Keith, who enjoyed nothing more than reading each chapter as it was being written and providing me with his insight and straightforward critique. And I thank my mother, Iris, who always taught me that perseverance and patience lead to good things.

While we worked on this project, traveling to all the cities where Eli was holding goaltending camps took me away from home for weeks on end. I thank my wife, Anna Marie, and my four adult children, Monet, Steven, Melanie, and Tyler, for keeping me focused and reminding me that with consistent effort I could complete a project of this magnitude. I would like to thank our contributing authors, Maria Mountain, Pete Fry, and Sonya DiBiase. Your efforts in writing these additional chapters were essential in making this a truly complete book of goaltending. I would also like to thank Peter Martin at Professional Skate Goalie Centre for supplying the equipment for our supplemental equipment photoshoot and Chris Gibbs of www.chrisgibbsphotography.com for supplying the photos.

I would like to thank all the good people at Human Kinetics, most notably the acquisitions editor, Diana Vincer, who always kept the ship pointed in the right direction, and the developmental editor, Laura Pulliam, whose brilliance and perceptiveness kept me on my toes and who truly put the finishing touches on this project.

Lastly, I want to thank Eli Wilson for having the faith in me to take all his knowledge of the goaltending position and put it down in words. Having known Eli for close to 15 years, I have watched him evolve from being a goalie coach in the Western Hockey League and running a goaltending school in Calgary, Alberta, Canada, to coaching in the NHL with the Ottawa Senators and building the Eli Wilson brand to what it is today. The hundreds of hours we spent together talking about the intricacies of the goaltending position and the hockey lifestyle in general are something I will cherish for the rest of my life.

—Brian

# Introduction

No other athletes in any sport are more passionate about everything to do with their position than the goaltenders in hockey. The equipment alone is more exciting than what any position in any other sport offers. Goaltenders agonize over picking the perfect gear with the best design and color-coordinated patterns. Their masks, sticks, gloves, skates, and pads must be just right. Choosing the equipment that satisfies a goaltender's needs for comfort, efficiency, protection, and appearance can be a daunting task. Goaltending is an obsession and an all-consuming lifestyle. Goaltenders are on a never-ending quest to stop more pucks, win more games, and lower their goals against averages.

On the other end of the spectrum, at the professional level, committees of people work tirelessly to figure out ways to increase scoring. Rule changes were made eliminating the center line to open the ice to create more offensive opportunities. Discussions have ranged from making the nets bigger to shrinking the goaltender's equipment. Yet year after year, average goals scored per game continue to dwindle. We believe the reason for this is that not only goaltenders but also coaches and equipment manufacturers put relentless thought and effort into making every aspect of the position better. There are so many passionate people who care, and that is why you see goaltending continuously evolving at a rapid pace.

The objective of this book is to simplify teaching the goaltending position. While most goalie coaches are looking to add tools to the goaltender's toolbox, we teach the opposite approach. We work with only the tools necessary to improve your game. We take out overcomplicated components to simplify your game and leave less margin for error. This book contains general philosophy as opposed to mass detail. We believe that a 10-year-old goaltender should be able to attain the same skills as a seasoned National Hockey League veteran. Obviously, the 10-year-old won't have the same speed and power as the pro, but he can have the same basic proficiency and knowledge of the position.

We always focus on things that are going to make a major difference in the goaltender's game regardless of what level he is playing. We don't nitpick on something that may stop two or three goals a year, but instead we focus on the things that will help the goaltender improve overall as an athlete and a goaltender. Contrary to what the highlight reel tends to depict, goaltending isn't all about making the big save. Consistency is the most important factor that sets the elite-level goaltender apart from the average.

We keep the game as simple as possible; our philosophy is that when a goaltender maintains proper position, he needs to extend his body only six inches in any direction to make a save. *Hockey Goaltending* contains everything the goaltender needs to know to elevate his game to the highest level.

Chapter 1, Selecting and Fitting Gear, is not just about selecting and fitting goaltending gear; we also focus on the engineered features built into each piece of equipment and the benefits provided for best fit and functionality. We analyze the complementary products that need to be considered that will provide the optimum performance to enhance the goaltender's overall game.

Chapters 2 and 3, Stance and Movement and Save Execution, take the goaltender through the full save process. Beginning with three types of stances, we show how to effectively navigate the crease while always providing the most net coverage. We discuss skating techniques to further enhance balance and mobility when moving in the crease. We explain the optimal techniques to employ when facing an actual shot. We analyze the butterfly save positions and the most opportune times to use each and continue on to proper execution of glove, blocker, stick, and pad saves. Chapter 4, Postsave Recovery, focuses on what to do after an initial save has been made. Where does the goaltender direct the puck? How does he set up for further play? Should he stay up or down? We analyze different types of rebounds and discuss strategy that will best prepare the goaltender for a second and a third shot.

Chapter 5, Puck Handling, focuses on the goaltender's role in handling the puck and assisting his teammates in clearing the defensive zone. Chapter 6, Tactics, looks at optimal tactics used by goaltenders to defend odd-man rushes, breakaways, shorthanded situations, penalty shots, screens, and deflections. Each tactical chapter comes complete with a set of on-ice drills that can be performed during team practices. The drills are designed to simulate gamelike situations with gray areas built in that will develop not only the goaltenders but all the players on the team. When developing a goaltender, goalie coaches need to build gray areas into drills so they are not producing cookie-cutter goaltenders. When drills are set to force the goaltender to read and react to unforeseen situations, the differences between the elite and average goaltender are exposed.

Chapter 7, Off-Ice Training, looks at ways to increase mobility through different methods of stretching. The chapter is chock-full of exercises to increase strength, speed, stamina, and agility for goaltenders. In-season and off-season training schedules are provided. What often separates successful goaltenders from the rest is their ability to apply mental toughness throughout the long season. Chapter 8, The Mental Game, discusses how to best prepare for games and what to do to overcome challenges that may arise throughout the season. Focus and visualization tactics along with when to apply each are discussed. We study game, season, and career goal setting and distinguish their differences.

We close the book with what may be one of the most important discussions. Chapter 9, Mentoring the Complete Goaltender, talks about the responsibilities of the goaltending coach, the head coach, and the goaltender and how all of them must coordinate to create a positive learning environment, which in turn will lead to improved success as a team. Good head coaches realize that without solid goaltending, they will not have a winning team, so they must build relationships with their goaltenders. Goalie coaches should not just act as a buffer between the goaltenders and the head coach. They have many other roles and responsibilities that are discussed in detail throughout the chapter. Ours goal is to reinforce the tactics that successful coaches are using and provide a guide to assist the less experienced.

*Hockey Goaltending* touches on every aspect of the position to give you, the goaltender, the best opportunity to compete at the highest levels of hockey. Work hard and enjoy every moment of the process, and remember, goaltending is not about luck; it's about skill.

# Chapter 1
# Selecting and Fitting Gear

## Sonya DiBiase

The equipment you choose to wear can significantly enhance your performance. You should view your equipment as one element of your tools to enhance your skills and improve your game. It is important to research the equipment options to better understand why equipment is designed a specific way and for whom the equipment is designed.

Goalie equipment is designed to protect the body. However, the advancements in engineered technology and specifications in goalie coaching and goalie development have allowed the design of goalie equipment to progress beyond protection to delivering performance benefits that improve your game by increasing your movement and efficiency in the crease.

One of the most important elements to consider when selecting any piece of goalie equipment is fit and how the gear interacts and reacts with your body. This reaction is most evident in the way the goalie pad rotates and drops to the ice as a reaction to your movements. The best pro-level goalie equipment available on the market today allows you to customize it to your fit, flexibility, and style of play. This is important because no two goalies have the same stature, flexibility, or playing style. Customizing your equipment provides the optimum fit and specifications for your style and how you move.

With fit being one of the most important elements in your equipment selection, it is important that when you make a product purchase, you always try on complementary pieces to ensure they fit together properly and are integrated. An excellent example of this is bringing your skates to the store or if you are purchasing new skates, wearing them when trying on goalie pads. It is important to simulate in the store how the equipment will be worn and ensure that all the products fit together and interact without restriction.

In this chapter, we focus on goalie protective equipment, the features and benefits that are designed and engineered into the products and how those features provide the best fit and performance. We discuss each product's purpose and functionality and highlight the complementary products that need to be considered to provide the optimum performance to enhance your skill. Much like goalie training, selecting the correct style and fit will take you from being satisfied with where you are today to exploring your potential and what you are able to achieve.

# GOALIE PADS

There are two types of goalie pads that are designed and engineered specifically for controlling the puck and preventing a goal. These two unique styles of goalie pads not only have visual differences on the front, but the complete design is engineered specifically for two different fits and styles. Historically, these two styles were called butterfly and hybrid. However, butterfly is a term for a save technique of dropping to the knees to cover the bottom of the net. This is only one technique of many that are taught in this book; therefore, all goaltenders are hybrid in the sense that they all use various save techniques to stop the puck.

The two styles of goalie pads we discuss are called the flat-face goalie pad and the knee-roll goalie pad, as these two attributes are the key visible differences. The flat-face goalie pad has one continuous plane from top to bottom, and the knee-roll goalie pad typically has three horizontal three-dimensional rolls running across the knee region.

## Flat-Face Goalie Pads

The flat-face goalie pads are designed for goalies who want to look big to cover more net (figure 1.1). The goaltender who prefers this style of goalie pads is looking for a big rebound to the corner and out of play to allow time to recover from dropping to his knees. Removing the traditional knee rolls, which creates the flat front, is done intentionally for controlling the rebound and directing the puck out of play. It is important that this style have a 60-degree boot angle, which provides directional control of the puck to the side instead of creating the juicy rebound in front that can provide a challenge for the second shot. The radius roll on the inside edge provides less drag on the ice when moving across the crease.

Many goalie pads are engineered with a core that consists of layered sheets of high- and low-density foam. Some companies use injection-molded foam to provide consistency and stability on the ice. The foam core allows customization of the flexibility of the goalie pads to create break points that are individual segments of the foam sheets. Goalie pads have three areas of internal foam core that can be adjusted for flexibility (figure 1.2). The most important area is the ankle, located directly between the lower shin and the top of the boot. The second flex area is below the knee, where the upper and lower vertical rolls are segmented. The third flex point (not all goalie pads feature this design) is above the knee, between the upper knee and thigh area. This flex point is requested only when goalies are looking for an extremely flexible goalie pad and prefer a tighter-fitting leg channel, which we will reference further in the knee-roll goalie pad.

The flat-face foam-core goalie pad usually consists of high-density foam on the top layer, closest to the front, which creates the big rebound and contributes to the stiffness of the pad. This design is engineered to have a stiffer top and a more flexible bottom ankle area. The stiffness begins at the knee and continues to the top of the thigh area. The stiffer top design creates a wall effect to maximize coverage and keep the puck in front of the goalie, and the goalie pad inside edge seals the ice to close the five-hole. The goalie pad is designed to have a thinner profile at the top to provide a deeper knee stance when in the butterfly position and the post-lean formation. The foam core from the bottom of the knee through the shin and into the boot area is engineered to be more flexible to allow goalies the ankle flexion for pushes and getting that optimum edge for an aggressive push angle.

It is important to note that since the goalie pad is stiffer in the top portion, the leg channel at the back of the goalie pad, including the knee cradle and calf area, needs to be styled with a looser fit. When the leg is locked into a tight-fitting leg

Figure 1.1    Flat-face goalie pad.

Figure 1.2    Internal foam core for customized flexibility.

channel with a stiffer design, the leg will be restricted, which could put more stress on the knees and hips. Many professional goalies who prefer the stiffer goalie pad often choose a knee cradle with no outside knee wrap because they prefer the fluid freedom of movement of the knee in the knee cradle and landing zone. The knee elastic is attached below the knee in the upper calf area to maximize the freedom of movement in the knee cradle.

When selecting a stiffer goalie pad design, it is important to ensure that your knee is in the center of the knee cradle and the leg straps are located at and below the knee. The top calf strap can have a direct correlation to drop velocity, as the strap becomes an end point to begin the momentum of the goalie pad dropping toward the ice. This same top calf strap can also improve recovery time, as the strap end point begins the momentum of returning to the stance. An elastic leg strap does not have tension; it extends when the leg moves without providing the end point. Therefore, it can allow the leg to move out of the leg channel and does not create the tension required to control the pad when dropping to the knees and when recovering.

Although goalie pads are designed with knee stacks to support the knee when on the ice, it is very important that you always wear a separate knee protector. There are many sizes and shapes of knee protectors, but the size you select should correlate with your leg-channel selection. For example, if you choose a loose-fitting leg channel, you can wear a larger knee protector. The body was not designed to drop on the knee 30 to 40 times in a 60-minute period. The knee stacks on all goalie pads do not provide enough protection to the knee joint when the knee is dropping to the ice. Therefore, the knee protector is designed to protect the knee joint from the impact of dropping on the ice as well as elevate the knees above the ankles when in the butterfly drop position to provide more flexibility in the hips.

The misconception is that the goalie who wears the stiffer goalie pad is extremely flexible; however, if you choose the proper loose-fitting leg channel on the stiffer goalie pad, it allows the knee and calf to move comfortably throughout the leg channel, and leg flexibility is required when practicing basic drills and performing save techniques.

## Knee-Roll Goalie Pads

The knee-roll goalie pad is designed with a three-dimensional front face, with knee rolls running horizontally across the knee section (figure 1.3). This pad is designed for goalies who are extremely agile when moving across the crease and want a softer pad that fits tightly to their leg so it feels as though it is an extension of them. This design is engineered with softer foam on the front of the pad to reduce the puck's velocity, which in turn reduces the rebound. The boot is engineered at a 90-degree angle to direct the puck in front of the goalie so it can be smothered. The flat inside edge provides a solid seal from the top to the bottom of the goalie pad and creates a stable landing area when dropping on your knees and moving across the crease.

The misconception is that the softer knee-roll goalie pad needs to have a double break, one below and one above the knee. However, many professional goalies still prefer a single break on the outer vertical roll but two breaks on the inside for horizontal flexion.

This goalie pad also features a thinner profile for the deeper knee stance, and often the knee cradle is recessed to provide a deeper fit. The calf wraps are often closer to the center of the back-leg channel to provide a tight fit, and an elastic strap is used to wrap and encompass the leg. Many professional goalies still use a cowhide leather or coated webbing top leg strap to provide the end point for faster drop velocity and recovery.

Although this goalie pad is designed for a tighter leg channel, it is still important for you to wear a knee protector to protect the knee from the impact of dropping; however, you may select a knee protector that is streamlined and contoured to wrap closer and tighter to the knee.

Regardless of which style of goalie pad you select, make sure you try on knee protectors and pants to ensure that all pieces work together and do not restrict your movement. The knee protector is a hinge and can often be connected inside the pants or from garter belts. Making sure that all components of your gear complement each other will limit distractions and help you focus on your game.

Figure 1.3　Knee-roll goalie pad.

# CATCH GLOVE

The catch glove is another important piece of equipment for your game (figure 1.4). Being able to catch the puck and close your glove around it is of utmost importance. There are several drills specific to hand positioning and

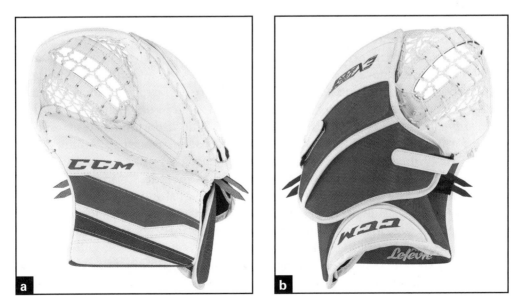

Figure 1.4　Catch glove: *(a)* front and *(b)* back.

eye-hand training. The glove is all about feel; it must feel comfortable and close easily.

Much like goalie pads, there are different closing breaks in all glove models. Some gloves, for example, close toward the fingers, and some close toward the thumb. One break is not better than the other; rather, the break is about comfort and forearm strength. Gloves are described as having either a 60- or 90-degree angle, which refers to the angle of the thumb.

The best way to know which break is best for you is to try the glove on in the store. Grab a stick and see how the glove feels when you simulate shooting the puck. Replicating how you use the equipment in the game will help you decide which product to choose.

Options are also offered in the tee pocket design. Much like the glove closure, the tee is a personal preference. The two common tee pocket styles are the single tee and the double tee, each providing its own benefits.

The single tee is often designed with a single synthetic leather region running from the top of the tee to the catch area with soft foam in the center of the tee to reduce the velocity of the puck when it enters the pocket. This tee has two lacing zones, one on each side of the center tee, and is available with skate or regular cord lacing.

The double tee features two synthetic leather regions with lacing between them to create three lacing zones. Most goalies prefer the double tee for its deep pocket and increased visibility from more lacing areas in which to see the puck, especially when smothering in front of the net. Although both regular and skate lacing are available in the double tee, because goalies want increased visibility, they select the regular lacing option, as the skate lacing is wider and can reduce visibility.

Advances in foam technology have made catch gloves more flexible without needing break-in periods. Foams having rate-sensitive properties are used to protect the hand in key sensitive areas.

Another option for catch gloves is the one- or two-piece cuff. A two-piece cuff allows the cuff to be independent of the catching surface and was designed to provide more flexibility at the wrist. With the advanced technology of composite materials in sticks, shots are getting faster and harder with quicker releases off the blade. These harder shots are being felt between the cuff and the catch area of the two-piece glove. This situation has created the need for a one-piece cuff, where the cuff and catch are integrated and provide more protection in the wrist and forearm areas.

Other great features available on catch gloves include a grip palm on the inside hand of the glove and adjustable straps to customize the fit. A Velcro strap at the finger stall area can secure the fingers and prevent slipping when closing the glove. It is important to also have adjustments at the back of the hand and the wrist. Usually, the wrist strap is kept loose to allow wrist flexibility, and the back-of-the-hand strap is secured tighter to provide solid hand positioning.

When selecting a catch glove, it is important to try on a chest protector to ensure that the opening of the cuff is wide enough for the forearm of a chest protector to rotate and move fluidly with the glove. The arm of the chest protector must be short enough to ensure the glove wrist straps can be secured without interference.

# BLOCKER

Some goalie equipment manufacturers will state that a blocker is just a blocker, but if you accept this philosophy, then you are overlooking some key features with performance benefits that can elevate your game.

The blocker is an extremely important piece of equipment because it must interact with the chest protector and the goalie stick (figure 1.5). The blocker must be lightweight because you are often playing with your hands up and out in front of your body; therefore, any weight reduction will reduce fatigue throughout the game.

Many blockers today feature high-performance impact foam and smart materials to protect the hand. Protecting the fingers is important when the puck rides up the paddle of the stick and hits the first finger that is placed straight on the paddle when holding the stick. The blocker can also provide more blocking surface beyond the face and front blocker board. The best

Figure 1.5　Blocker.

pro goalies today use blockers that provide a large inside thumb and cuff protectors that not only protect the hand and wrist but also provide more blocking surface.

When purchasing a blocker, it is important to try on a chest protector to confirm the arm fits into the blocker cuff. Some blockers are available with an adjustable cuff to increase the opening for the chest-protector arm. It is also important to put a goalie stick in your hand and get the feel of the grip and protection wrapping around the fingers. The blocker may feel stiff when it is new in the store, but the foams are moldable. After the first few times on the ice, the finger foams will mold and shape around the paddle of the stick.

# CHEST PROTECTOR

Like goalie pads, chest protectors are available in two styles: squared, for goalies who want to look big to cover more net (figure 1.6a), and angular, for goalies who want to maximize their mobility in the crease (see figure 1.6b). The style you select may slightly affect the amount of protection you get, but some goalies are willing to sacrifice a little protection to maximize their movements in the crease.

If you want to look big and maximize your coverage, you need to look for models that have more square edges around the shoulder area and the arms. The human body has round shoulders, but through design and pattern engineering, some chest protectors have square corners to maximize blocking surface without restricting movement. The square design still provides mobility, as all the patterns work in an armadillo design to overlap and not interfere with lateral movements.

The most important areas of protection in the chest protector are the clavicle and sternum. The front midchest area is often positioned away from the body so that if the puck were to hit your chest, the air between the protector and your body would absorb the energy and protect your body from a direct impact. Often in a game, you use your glove or blocker to catch or deflect the puck in the midabdominal area, so the upper chest area is the most vulnerable. Look for a chest protector that has smart foam with high-impact absorption in the upper-chest section, and always wear a certified neck protector under your chest protector. There are also base layer performance padded shirts that can be worn under the chest to provide additional protection in the sternum and kidney regions. This padded shirt is a great addition and can be used in a practice where the goalie is faced with more shots on net.

© chrisgibbsphotography.com

Figure 1.6   Chest protector: *(a)* squared design and *(b)* angular design.

# PANTS

Goalie pants are designed to maximize your coverage and protect the thigh and groin areas; today, however, many designs are engineered with unique features to make you look big and increase your mobility (figure 1.7). The pants need to integrate with the chest protector, the knee protector, and the goalie pads. Always consider the base layer and jock protection that will be worn under the pants. You will need to consider whether you tuck in your chest protector or wear it outside the pants. If you tuck in the chest protector, you will want to open the top of your pants wider by adjusting the belts and lacing.

Figure 1.7   Goalie pants.

Always look for goalie pants that fit well without restricting mobility. The best goalies in the world work to develop their leg muscles and speed, so you do not want the goalie pants to impede your mobility.

The inner belt allows a snug fit, and the outer shell is positioned away from the body so you can still look big in the net and maximize your coverage. Many goalie pants feature thin smart materials to maximize mobility but still offer high-impact absorption on those harder shots.

The one-inch-length extender is a new feature to look for when making a goalie pants purchase. A placket of extra material hidden behind a zipper along the waistband allows an additional one to two inches of length in the waist-to-hem measurement. This is a great feature for young goalies who are growing throughout the season.

# MASK

Often, goalies spend more time researching goalie pads than they do researching goalie masks. The mask is the most important piece of protection you wear (figure 1.8). The game is fast, and the rushes to the net can often cause interference with the goalie. It is important to protect your brain not only from a puck's impact but also from a collision on the ice or with other players.

The mask is a challenging product to design, as there are many head shapes and sizes. It is important that the mask fits the head and that it is anchored at the chin cup. The more toward the front of the mask the face sits, the greater the peripheral vision. When you have better vision, not only are you able to track the puck, but you also can see the play around you and be aware of any pucks, sticks, elbows, or any other objects that could impact your head.

Pro masks on the market are approved by the Hockey Equipment Certification Council (HECC), Canadian Standards Association (CSA), and CE (Conformité Européenne). They have

Figure 1.8    Goalie mask.

composite materials in the shell that absorb energy and a foam liner, which also provides protection and is important for ensuring your mask fits properly so the protection is in the correct position.

Often, a goalie will have a cracked mask or a bent cage, and the assumption is that the mask or cage was defective. What it indicates, though, is that the mask did its job by absorbing the impact and it is no longer certified and needs to be replaced. If the cage does not bend, then the impact energy will often be transferred to the head and the brain.

The mask should never be altered. However, if you have your mask painted, always ensure that you are working with a certified painter who understands the CSA and HECC regulations and is using paints that will not damage the integrity of the shell.

Make sure you are properly fitted for your mask. The back plate and elastic straps should be loose so your face is placed inside the mask with your chin properly positioned in the chin cup. Many masks provide adjustability in the chin, which is important because the chin anchors the mask. The mask should fit snugly without any gaps between the forehead and cheek area and the inner foam. The bars of the cage should not impede your vision, and there should be an inch or two between your nose and the cage. After the mask has been properly positioned, the back plate should be secured with the snaps and the elastic adjusted so the back plate is inside the shell.

It is also recommended to wear a Lexan throat protector that can be attached with a lacing rope on the side of the mask. The Lexan throat protector dangles from the mask and provides mobility.

# SKATES

Good goaltenders are great skaters, and the best goaltenders have the skill to move quickly and effortlessly on their feet. There are three things to look for in a skate: proper fit, protection, and attack angle.

Proper fit is important; comfort will be an important benefit of a proper fit when you consider the amount of time you spend standing stationary until the play is in your zone. A heat-moldable, high-performance skate is a great feature to have for a true customized fit (figure 1.9). An asymmetrical cuff on a skate can provide more flexion when you are deep in your stance or in the power push, and it can also assist with recovery to stand up. High-performance skates offer moisture-wicking materials in the boot liner to keep feet dry and skates light throughout the game. A foot bed that offers aeration vents will provide excellent foot-to-skate contact and comfort.

Protection is important. Even though you see some goalies, such as Carey Price, removing their boot straps to allow more mobility, this can often leave the skate exposed. Because companies are engineering boots to reduce weight by reducing or removing the cowling, it is important to ensure that your skate boot be constructed with high-performance composite materials with strategic reinforcements where goalies could receive a shot. The toe

© chrisgibbsphotography.com

Figure 1.9   A heat-moldable, high-performance goalie skate.

area would be one of those strategic areas that you need to ensure is well protected because this is the most exposed area of the skate and is often directly impacted by the puck. Boots are engineered with composite materials for protection and to reduce weight in the skate. The felt tongue is a great feature for reducing lace bite. Look for smart materials added to the felt tongue to reduce the weight and provide additional lace-bite protection when in the forward-flexed position.

The cowlingless and low-profile cowling skates are both options for reducing weight and achieving the aggressive attack angle you desire. These cowlings, with the addition of a taller high-performance blade, translate to not needing to raise your knees as high or lift the goalie pad as far off the ice, which allows for quicker movements. There are also blades on the market with coatings and treatments for longer life and increased resistance to corrosion.

When selecting a skate, always be sure you are properly fitted. Attach your goalie pads to the skates and replicate your stance to ensure that the goalie pads rotate properly with the skates.

# STICK

The goalie stick is another important tool for improving your game. It is important that you have the correct stick length for your height and stance. Often, goalies use sticks that are too long, which can add unnecessary weight and put the blocker too far away from the body to create a hole or gap for scoring. Contrarily, sticks should not be too short. If they are, you will not be able to position the blade on the ice, and the blocker will not work as an additional blocking surface but will instead overlap the goalie pad and chest area. When purchasing a goalie stick, it is important that you have your blocker in hand and wear your skates with your pads so you can determine the proper stick length for your height and stance.

Regardless of your goaltending style or how often you like to play the puck, two stick constructions are available: foam core and composite (figure 1.10). Foam-core sticks today are made from a combination of foam and composite.

Foam-core sticks are engineered with wood, foam reinforcements, and composite materials. The main performance benefit of a foam-core stick is the foam reinforcement within the paddle to dampen the vibration from the puck. Graphite and other composite materials are added throughout the stick handle, paddle, and blade to reduce weight and add consistency, performance, and durability. Many goalies in the NHL prefer foam-core sticks because of the "feel" they provide them.

Composite goalie sticks are made entirely of composite materials, creating the lightest stick option on the market. Different composite materials are used in specific areas to reduce vibration and stiffen the blade. The stiffer blade is designed to deflect the puck accurately where you want to send it.

Figure 1.10    Goalie sticks: *(a)* foam core and *(b)* composite.

Much testing is done in the development phase to ensure optimum feel and control of the puck.

Blade curves are designed for performance. Although you may want to play with the curve that your favorite NHL goalie uses, it may not be the best curve for you. A medium-size heel curve, which is very open, is designed to clear the zone, often in the air or off the glass. A big heel curve, which is slightly open, is deeper to help move the puck quickly. A medium midcurve position in the center of the blade is slightly open and is great for controlling the puck around the net.

Whether purchasing pads, mask, gloves, stick, or any other piece of equipment, always be sure to size it properly and choose the gear that best suits your style of play. Improperly fitted gear will lead to negative results on the ice for any goaltender. The equipment you wear must always offer the utmost in protection while providing you both comfort and mobility.

# Chapter 2

# Stance and Movement

How often have you heard broadcasters, coaches, and fans say, "The goaltender didn't have any challenging saves today!" It often happens, and although that comment can be upsetting to a goaltender, it is in fact the highest of compliments. Many coaches overcomplicate the goaltending position with fancy terms and inefficient drills, but the key for successful goaltenders is to keep their game simple and efficient.

All the great goalies in the game today (e.g., Carey Price, Braden Holtby, Pekka Rinne, and Corey Crawford) have one thing in common—the ability to make most of their saves look easy. Goaltenders of yesteryear made an enormous number of saves by stacking the pads or kicking out a skate. Although these saves may have looked scintillating to broadcasters and fans alike, they were completely inefficient. Those movements are not effective on a consistent basis because the goaltender puts himself so much out of position in making the first save that he is unable to recover for a rebound. Limiting movements and being efficient in the movements they make are what separate elite goaltenders from the rest.

Simplicity and efficiency are the keys for goaltenders to rise above their competition. This concept will be reiterated numerous times throughout this book. Pick any goaltending book off the shelf, and chances are you will find a chapter on how to stand in the net and move from position to position on the ice. You probably haven't thought about this since you were a youngster in goalie school. Often, those kinds of chapters get a cursory glance, and then readers move on. Instead, we suggest you study this chapter, as proper stance and efficient movement are the key building blocks to successful goaltending (save position and postsave recovery are covered in chapter 3). Along with stance and movement, we discuss head-first–stick-first goaltending, path of direction, and hard and soft focus. Let's begin with the stance.

# STANCE

Since the inception of goaltending, instructors have aimed to perfect a basic stance and movement, and for good reason. Stance and movement together are the basis for shot preparation. Together, they drive and reflect your mental state—your preparation, level of focus, and most of all, attitude.

All athletes begin from a fundamental athletic position and base their performance on sound foundational skills. The technical aspects of their sport are built upon this solid foundation. Goaltending is no different; in fact, it may apply here even more than in most other sports. Although how we read the play and (at more advanced levels) how we influence the play are key, we are fundamentally responding in a read-and-react manner to what comes to us. Being prepared, being able to get into position early, and being ready to respond separate elite goaltenders from the rest.

For every goaltender, what that stance looks like will be different. Bodies are different; some are taller, some are smaller, some are longer in the leg, and some are longer in the upper body. Every goaltender will have different angles and varying degrees of flexibility and strength upon which to build his stance. However, the basic elements that make up an effective stance are universal—a set position that is low, explosive, and balanced, which allows the goaltender to move forward, backward, side to side, and up and down with as much ease as possible. Combined with the need to provide balance and efficiency, the goalie must choose a stance that is comfortable. You will see slight variations of stance as the goaltender adjusts to find the perfect level of comfort in his chosen stance.

Your stance is not simply a starting point. Layered on top of those basics, you are crafting your own unique identity. Are you passive or aggressive? Do you choose a stance that is more athletic or one that provides more net coverage? The stance reflects your mindset on the ice and your approach to the game—even a situation within the game. And this is not simply a passive reflection. The stance you take in any situation drives the attitude you take to the game. Your attitude is reflected by your basic stance as much as your stance is affected by your approach to the game. Take control of your attitude from the first position that you take on the ice. This is not to say that you must always be in an aggressive, fired-up position. There are situations that call for a more relaxed, passive attitude. As you move into your stance, have a mental picture of what you are trying to accomplish, and let your stance both reflect and influence that result.

The stance is built around several basics; however, some of these basics will be adjusted in different tactical situations. We are now going to look at five basic stances: the regular stance, the tall stance, the low stance, the blocker-side post stance, and the glove-side post stance.

# The Regular Stance

The regular stance (figure 2.1) is mostly used when you are set to face a shot or scoring chance. An ideal regular stance is one that allows you to maximize efficiency while staying comfortable. It is essentially a ready position to do anything, whether moving to a different location in the crease or reacting to a shot.

## Feet

Foot positioning is the most important aspect of the regular stance. It is suggested that you take a stance with your feet positioned slightly more than shoulder-width apart. The ideal foot placement is slightly wider than your shoulder width. This position allows you to dig the blades into the ice at the proper angle. Because the feet are not positioned too far apart, it will be quick and easy for you to bring them into a position to generate maximum power.

While an even wider stance has evolved over the years and may be used in some tactical situations, keep in mind that having your feet under you and your legs bent provides a strong foundation for lateral movement. Clearly, lateral movement is not efficient with the legs immediately under the shoulders,

Figure 2.1    The regular stance.

but a point is reached where that movement is impaired by an excessively wide stance and a wide angle between the hips and body. So find the position in your stance that provides both comfort and efficient lateral movement.

It is important to avoid positioning your feet too close together or too far apart for the following reasons:

- If you keep both feet close together underneath your body, you will not get the skate blade to the angle needed to execute the push, and you more than likely will slip.

- If your feet are too close together, you will not be able to execute the butterfly properly, which in turn will impede your ability to stop pucks (more about this in chapter 3). You would also take too much time pushing your feet to the outside to cover the lower portion of the net.

- If you did not move your feet to the outside and were simply to push your hips forward, you would leave the lower corners of the net wide open.

- Having your feet too wide will hinder your ability to recover from a save and control a rebound.

## Knees

When in the regular stance, you should bend your knees. This allows you to place your feet at the desired width. If your knees are straight, then your feet will automatically set underneath your body, bringing about the negative results we discussed previously. Having bent knees brings you lower to the ice, which improves your reaction time to get into a butterfly position.

## Torso

Just like foot position, the position of your torso will affect mobility. If your torso is too straight, it will throw off your center of gravity, shifting it back slightly behind your body. As a result, you will easily lose your balance and will eventually find yourself on your backside. Balance is an essential component for reacting to quick and sometimes awkward plays. A lack of balance limits your chances for success.

You should lean your upper body forward with your "nose over toes." The chest is upright with the lean coming from the hips. The shoulders should be held back with the chest out. You must avoid rounding your shoulders and upper back forward because that will result in negative consequences. Your balance will be compromised as will your ability to reach with your arms. Just like the hips, the elbows should be bent at an angle. This allows maximum power from the shoulder, upper back, and arm muscles. Maintaining this angle provides the perfect balance between tightness and the ability to react. Keeping the elbows bent automatically sets the forearms and gloves a few inches above the hips and thighs. We cannot overemphasize proper posture while playing goal.

One evolution we now see is a more pronounced forward lean of the torso. In the days dominated by a blocking mindset, coaches wanted their goaltenders to play as upright as possible, and many still do today, mistakenly believing goaltenders will cover more of the upper portion of the net this way. From the eye of a coach or another player, this may indeed appear true, but from the puck's perspective it is not. A little basic geometry may help you understand (figure 2.2). Stand in the slot with a goaltender in the net, and look at how much open net you see. Now, lie down on the ice at the level of the puck and note how much less open net you see. Remember, the puck must find an opening on the goaltender before it can make its way into the net.

The optimal stance for a goalie is very much like that of athletes in other sports. Your body is designed in such a way that for you to generate as much power as possible and attain optimal mobility and balance, your hips must be back enough so your thighs and torso are angled. From that position, you can use your core muscles to their maximum and generate ultimate power. Examples of athletes from other sports who try to achieve this position are tennis players and batters in baseball. Karate experts also push their hips forward, powering their punches and kicks with hip rotation.

## Stick

The stick is always held in front of the body on the ice; however, its position over the years has also evolved. No longer held close to the feet and upright, it is now held in front of the body so the blade can be seen in the goaltender's peripheral vision. In front, the stick can be used with more dexterity and access more pucks laterally while directing low shots out of danger and absorbing them as needed. The stick will not interfere as a goaltender drops into the butterfly and is always at the ready to retrieve or deflect pucks out of harm's way.

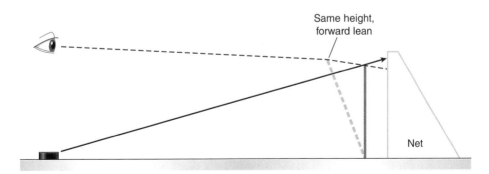

Figure 2.2   Covering the net from the puck's perspective.

The stick is a major balance point of the stance and is used to drive movement whether moving forward off the post or laterally from side to side. You want to be a "stick-first" goaltender. When moving forward, your hands and stick drive out as a guide. The same thing is true when moving laterally; the stick is used as a balance and a drive point to move into position.

## Hands

The term "active hands" is relatively new, although the concept of a forward-hand position is not. In fact, where goaltenders hold their hands today is relatively no different than where they held them in the 1990s. You should hold your hands forward of your trunk. This position gives you a peripheral view of your gloves and allows access to pucks in more positions both beside and in front of your body. It is important to avoid covering net already shielded by your body, called double coverage, by holding your gloves in front of and outside of your body.

Like the legs and trunk, a forward-hand position is about being more athletic. By athletic, we are not referring to one goalie being a better athlete than another; rather, we are using the term to refer to being in a ready position. Recognize that along with your stick, your glove is the best way to control pucks. A more forward, ready position allows you to use your hands to access and control more pucks—to the point that we see goaltenders catching pucks today at near ice level or across and in front of their bodies. A major key to success is your awareness of your hands. When moving, always think about hand position. Your hands will tend to drop out of position to make saves when you are not fully aware of them.

Just like the stance, the glove position is up to you, but it must be based on principles and basics that allow you to get to and control pucks. The glove position also changes according to tactical situations, which we discuss later in the book in Chapter 3 on Save Execution.

# The Tall Stance

The tall stance (figure 2.3) is used when the play does not pose an immediate threat. The goaltender stays in a more upright position than in the regular stance. The idea behind this stance is that you can conserve energy and at the same time have a greater field of vision. There are several instances when the tall stance is optimal:

- When you first leave the goal line to meet a rush, or when the puck is close to the walls or at the blue line so there is no immediate danger of a scoring opportunity.
- When you face a shorthanded situation, the play often stays in the zone for a long time. This stance allows you to regain composure as the puck moves back to the blue line.
- Any time there is a lot of traffic in front of the net.

Figure 2.3   The tall stance.

The main technical difference between the regular and tall stances is foot positioning. The goaltender places his feet shoulder-width apart in the tall stance, whereas in the regular stance, he places his feet slightly wider than shoulder width. By bringing the feet closer together, the goaltender can now straighten his body and bring his hips forward. The arms and gloves should not move. The goaltender's stick will come up off the ice.

The key to utilizing the tall stance is that the goalie can get back into his regular stance in a split second. He must slightly push his feet to the outside, allowing them to go beyond shoulder width. He must then draw his hips back. The arms and gloves should already be set in the proper position. As the goaltender gets lower, his stick should be back on the ice in optimal position. Although the goaltender is not in an optimal ready position when using the tall stance, he is only a split second away from assuming that position. Here are a few more advantages of using the tall stance:

- You can easily stay square to the puck. In a tall and narrow position, you can be precise at lining up the middle of your body with the puck.
- A tall stance increases your mobility. If the opposition performs cross-ice D-to-D passes, you can follow the play by executing long, hard pushes. When the puck comes in tight, you are just a split second away from adjusting back to your regular stance and performing a butterfly movement.
- When in the tall stance, you have a greater field of view. You can track the puck by looking over and around players when there is a lot of

traffic in front. In most circumstances, it is easier to watch the puck while standing up higher than it is from a low, crouched position. You must have the ability to quickly drop back into your regular stance and be able to go down to make the save.

## The Low Stance

In contrast to the tall stance, the low stance (figure 2.4) is used for situations in tight to the goaltender, where he is required to bring his center of gravity down. To drop into the low stance, you must completely do the opposite of the tall stance by pushing your feet out into a wider position and bringing your hips back.

This will bring your body closer to the ice and thus put you in a position where you can react faster. Again, your arms and hands should not be moving. Your elbows should be kept close to your ribs, and you should be in full control of your forearms. Occasionally, you might have to push your arms slightly forward to adjust your upper body to the new, lower position. By doing so, you will be able to keep your arms close to your body, hips, and thighs.

When the play is in tight, the goaltender's reaction time to make a save is greatly reduced. Following are some of the advantages of dropping into the low stance:

Figure 2.4  The low stance.

- Bringing your knees closer to the ice makes the transition to the butterfly position much quicker.
- Having your knees close to the ice when the play is in close is advantageous, as chances for a shot to the lower part of the net are very high.
- Although being in a wider stance decreases your power and mobility, the fact that the play is in tight means you will be deeper in your crease. If you must move, your pushes will not need to be as long as when you are at the top of your crease, so you can still get across to make the save.

# Post Stances

Post stances are the foundation to defend all plays that take place down low or below the red line. You must be able to quickly adjust to stop potential scoring threats, including wraparounds, net drives, and passes out front.

Because of the increased speed of offensive attacks down low, it is extremely important that you can move uninhibitedly from the post to defend any scoring chances that arise in front of you. Terms being bandied around the coaching ranks, such as "post integration," have overcomplicated what it means to gain proper post coverage. The keys to successfully guarding the post on the blocker and glove sides are outlined next.

## Blocker-Side Post Stance

We cannot overemphasize the importance of being in a ready position from the post. The only things you will do from the post position are to get wide and into a shoulder-lean position (shoulder leans are discussed in detail in chapter 4) or move in your crease to defend a scoring opportunity.

The following are the keys to defending the post on the blocker side:

- Have a tight seal and be in a ready position with the chest up and the body slightly bent toward the post so you can move from your post position easily (figure 2.5). You want to avoid "hugging" the post, as this will lock you in at the post and you will not be able to move off your post quickly to defend plays as they develop in front of you.
- The heel of your skate is tight to the inside of the post, which in turn butts the pad up to the post, and the heel of your stick butts up to the toe of your post skate. Your shoulder is set against the post, and your head is bent slightly downward so your eyes are down over the puck.
- The stick must be tight. If sealing to the post on the blocker side, you want to have the heel of your stick against the toe of your skate. Note that there are also occasions when you will turn the blade of your stick to face the puck below the goal line to deter a pass.

Figure 2.5    The blocker-side post stance.

- Carry your hands, which means keeping your elbows in tight to your body and thus flaring your hands out into a ready position. When your elbows are tight to your body, your hands are strong and in position. Your hands should always be a focal point of what you do as a goaltender. A constant awareness of your hands as you move around in your crease is essential. Make sure your head is forward over your toes and angled down, as we mentioned previously. That way you are always playing over the puck.

- Keep your back leg adjustable depending on where the play moves (we discuss this more thoroughly in chapter 3).

- Maintain balance and be ready to move.

## Glove-Side Post Stance

Much like the blocker side, when defending the post on the glove side, you want to be in a lean position on the post with your chest up and head in a downward position looking over the puck. It is important to maintain a tight seal on the post but not be locked into position so you can move off the post easily as the play develops in front of you.

The following are the keys to defending the post on the glove side:

- Have a tight seal and be in a ready position with the chest up and head angled downward looking over the puck so you can track the play around you (figure 2.6).

Figure 2.6　The glove-side post stance.

- Make sure your hands are up and in a ready position and you are holding your stick firmly.
- The outside of your heel should be butted up firmly to the post.
- The stick must be tight. If sealing the post on the glove side, the toe of your stick is set tight against the toe of your post skate, or you can position the heel of your stick against the toe of your skate.
- Hold the stick tightly so a puck can't be banked off the stick and into the net. The glove hand must remain adjustable. There is no right or wrong way (palm out or palm in) to hold the glove.
- Use the back leg as a steering mechanism to pull yourself through the center of the net.
- Maintain balance and be ready to move.

# MOVEMENT

Movement is the foundation of goaltending. Goaltenders and players don't skate the same, and for that reason it is essential that you master movement and edge control through regular skating and movement work. Watch an NHL practice, and you will see goaltenders perfecting their movement doing the very same motions that beginner goalies use and practice. This is because movement is fundamental to their craft, and perfection is their goal.

This portion of the chapter focuses on all the key components required for a goaltender to move properly and with purpose. We discuss the concepts of head-first–stick-first goaltending, hard and soft focus, and path of direction.

# Head-First–Stick-First Goaltending

The theory behind this concept is simple: everything must go forward. Whenever moving from one location to another, you lead with your head, with your hands and stick as a guide. You should simply turn your head, keeping your chin downward, and drive to the destination while keeping your hands and stick out front and using the stick as a balance point. Do not pull back out of position to move to your destination. Take everything from one position into the next. What this means is that you do not move your body out, back, or away from your destination. Goaltenders were once taught to load up all their power onto their back leg and then push off to their destination. Notice what happens with your upper body as you load up? See how it moves back as your weight shifts onto your back leg? We want you to move directly into position without loading up by keeping your eyeballs centered, turning your head, and simply moving into the desired position on the ice. Lead with your head every time!

# Hard and Soft Focus

Hard focus is the goaltender's concentration and focus on the puck and the puck only. It is of utmost importance to always know where the puck is. Without keeping a keen eye on the puck's location, you will often find it in the back of the net.

Soft focus is a hockey sense and awareness that can be taught to a beginning goaltender while working on skating drills. At the NHL level, a goaltender may use soft focus hundreds of times in a game, scanning and looking for certain plays that could potentially occur. You start on one side of the ice, push and stop on the other side, and take a quick look across from where you came to scan the ice for the next play. For example, let's assume a shooter in the faceoff circle to your left passes the puck to a shooter in the faceoff circle to your right. You want to beat the pass to the shooter on the right and then take a quick glance back to your left to see whether the shooter to your left has moved.

# Path of Direction

In basic terms, path of direction means you are always moving through the center of the crease to get to your next position on the ice—always taking away the middle of the net as early as possible. The common belief is that the fastest way to move between two points is a straight line, and although this is mostly true, it is not the desired result a goalie is trying to achieve. Rather than trying to get to your next destination as quickly as possible, you are trying to cover the middle of the net as quickly as possible.

When you push in straight lines, you are often exposing yourself on the short side until you are in an ideal position. Pushing in straight lines means that you will expose the center of the net longer while moving from point A to point B. The path of direction is all about gaining net coverage as quickly as possible. The key is to chase space, not the puck.

Look at figure 2.7. If you are standing at the top corner of the blue paint and shooter A passes across the ice to shooter B, pay attention to what happens if you were to drive in a straight line (line 1) to the opposite side of the crease. Notice how far you must move before you start filling space in the net. Now, look at what happens when you circle back through the middle of the crease (line 2). You go in a slight backward direction to fill the middle of the net sooner and then continue to your desired position on the ice. This allows you to start covering more of the net sooner than the previous method.

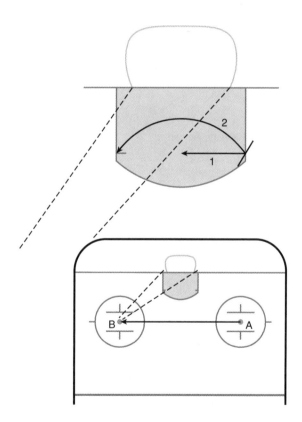

**Figure 2.7** The goaltender moves back and cuts through the middle of the crease to achieve faster and increased net coverage.

In figure 2.8, the puck is passed out of the corner from player A into the center to player B. Line 1 shows what happens when the goaltender pushes out in a straight line. Notice how much more quickly net coverage begins in the movement represented by line 2. In this movement, the goalie cuts through the center of the crease, taking away more of the net earlier. In movement number 1, by pushing straight out, the goaltender leaves more of the net exposed for a longer time.

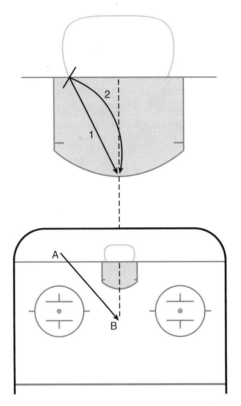

**Figure 2.8** The goaltender cuts through the center of the crease and gains net coverage faster than if moving in a straight line.

# SKATING AND MOVEMENT TECHNIQUES

Skating for a goaltender is the foundation of being able to move properly, get into position, and make saves. We will run through three skating skills: the C-cut, the T-push, and the shuffle. Take the time to continually work on these techniques and hone your skills during practice or any goalie-specific sessions.

# C-Cut

C-cuts are the most basic forward and backward movement used by a goal-tender throughout a game. They are primarily used to back into the net or to gain depth. The C-cut can also be used to adjust a goaltender's square-ness or direction. Considerable power can be generated with a short, quick movement while remaining in a stance. Movements can be executed without any perceptible change in upper-body position, always remaining ready to make a save.

When performing the C-cut, the heel of the goalie's lead skate comes back toward the body by cutting through the ice in a "C" figure. As the heel is coming back to the body, the goaltender opens his ankle toward the puck and lets the toe point at the new angle. The goalie lets his back foot pivot. As we mentioned above, the back foot rotates in such a way that the inside of the blade faces the puck. While the lead foot opens toward the puck, the back skate also slightly changes direction and rotates toward the puck.

When executing a forward C-cut, the goaltender turns the toe outward and pushes down and forward on the back inside edge. Then, he returns the push leg into a regular stance position as quickly as possible. For a backward C-cut, the goaltender turns the toe inward and pushes down and forward on the front inside edge before returning the push leg into a regular stance position as quickly as possible.

---

### Goaltender Tips: C-Cut

- Point the lead foot straight at the puck.
- Bring the lead foot back close to the body.
- Make sure the feet are not too far apart.
- Generate power from the hip.
- Keep the head up.

# T-Push

The T-push is the most common skating movement used by goaltenders. It is used for lateral movement, forward movement off the post, and retreating to the post. In fact, it is used almost every time the puck is passed.

Since the T-push is used for long-distance movements, the goalie will be required to rotate his body before pushing (figure 2.9). He does this to reposition himself so he can attack a new angle produced by the puck's ever-changing position. When the T-push is properly executed, the goaltender's feet take the shape of a T. When the T formation is created, it must be done in a way to ensure the inside of the lead skate is parallel to the puck and the toe of that same skate is pointing perpendicular to the new angle cre-

Figure 2.9 T-push.

ated by the new puck position. This means that the lead skate will now be pointing at the position where the goaltender wants to end up. Do not draw the lead skate toward the push skate for power. Just push straight toward your destination.

**Goaltender Tips: T-Push**

- Always lead with the head (chin pointed down) and stick.
- Keep the hands balanced.
- Stop hard on the lead skate.
- Keep the shoulders level.
- Track the puck.

## Shuffle

The shuffle is used for short side-to-side movements so a goaltender can remain with his chest centered on the puck while tracking the puck carrier. For instance, when an opposing player breaks in on goal and stickhandles in on the goalie, the goaltender will have to slightly adjust his position to stay square to the shooter. To react to a series of small positional adjustments by a shooter and the possibility of a shot, the T-push is not the right choice. Those situations require that the goaltender be ready, square to the puck, and in control of his speed and movements. Therefore, the short movements of the shuffle are ideal.

The execution of a shuffle is different than that of the T-push for two reasons. First, unlike the T-push, the goaltender keeps both of his toes pointing at the puck. Second, the back skate is not used to generate power. The goaltender will use his lead skate to initiate the movement. The shuffle is a technique in which the goaltender reaches toward where he wants to go, not pushing toward the puck. As the play moves sideways, the goaltender follows in a sideways pattern with his lead skate initiating the movement.

Every time the goaltender reaches with his lead skate, he must bring his back leg toward his body. It is essential that the back skate come underneath close to the goalie's body so that between each shuffle, he is back in his initial stance. If the goaltender does not move his back foot in a crisp manner, he will gradually end up with a too-wide stance. A wide stance will make it very difficult to continue moving. Since power comes from underneath the body, it is essential for the goalie to keep his feet under his body so he can garner maximum power in his shuffles.

### Goaltender Tips: Shuffle

- Keep the feet forward and the knees bent.
- Push off inside edge of trailing skate.
- Keep shoulders level.
- Keep the head up.
- Maintain regular stance throughout the movement.
- Stay square to the shooter.

# STANCE AND MOVEMENT DRILLS

As you move, are you remaining in your stance with legs bent, hands forward, and stick on the ice and in the middle? Do your head and shoulders remain stationary, or do they bob up and down? Except for turning the head to locate and track the target, when you move, there should be no indication above the waist that you are moving at all. Where are your eyes? Are they up and tracking the puck or staring down at the ice? Your head and eyes should be tracking imaginary pucks in set positions on the ice.

While not all practice drills are designed with the goalie in mind, we hope there will be an inherent understanding as to how drills can be structured to support goaltending development. In chapter 3, we discuss specific movements that goaltenders execute after every save to be prepared for the next shot. Adding those drills into team practices affords goalies the opportunity to follow and play rebounds and allows them to work on all their skills. All movement drills provided here give goaltenders the opportunity to focus on stance, skating, balance, movement (path of direction), soft focus, and post position.

# Post and Out Drill

## Purpose

This drill allows the goaltender to work on movement.

## Setup

There are no shooters required for this drill. The goaltender starts at the top of the crease in the center.

## Instructions

1. Start at the center top of the crease in a strong, regular stance.
2. Turn head, turn shoulders, rotate, and utilizing the T-push, push directly to the post.
3. Stop in a set post stance. Have a quick look to the slot using soft focus.
4. Using path of direction, push through the middle of the crease back to the original starting position, stopping on the lead leg at the top center of the crease.
5. Using the same technique as in step 2, turn and push to the other post. Take a quick look to the back door using soft focus.

## Coaching Tips

- Treat all movements as game situations.
- Always ensure that the stop is hard, matching the force of the push. Push hard and stop hard every time!
- Keep head in an upright position. Do not keep head in a fixed position. When coming to a stop, quickly look so you can see the play developing around you. For all your movement drills, create good habits utilizing soft focus.

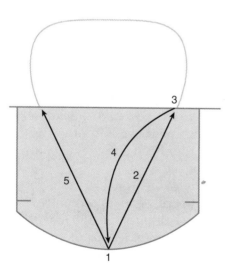

# Three-Stop Box Drill

## Purpose

This drill allows the goaltender to work on all the skills performed in the previous drill. This drill also forces the goaltender to practice good depth positioning while leading with his head and carrying his hands through the movements, including short, explosive T-pushes.

## Setup

The goaltender starts in a set position at the post.

## Instructions

1. Using soft focus, quickly look to the slot.
2. Turn head, turn shoulders, rotate, and use the T-push to move to the top corner of the crease.
3. Stop on the lead leg in a set position.
4. Rotate, turn, and push to the top center of the crease.
5. Stop at the top of the crease in a set position.
6. Turn and push to the opposite top corner of the crease.
7. Stop in set position.
8. Turn and push to the other post.
9. Stop in a set position on the post. Using soft focus, quickly look at the back door.

## Coaching Tips

- Always lead with your head and stick when moving from one position to another.
- Drive with your stick. When leading with your stick, keep your hands in front of your body.
- Come to a complete stop between each movement.

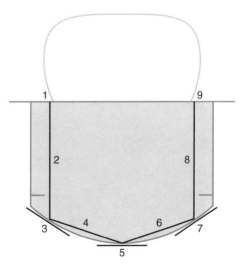

# Two-Stop Box Drill

## Purpose

This drill is like the previous drill; however, instead of stopping in the middle of the crease, the goaltender goes from one corner at the top of the crease to the other corner, utilizing path of direction. This drill introduces long T-pushes.

## Setup

The goaltender starts in a set position at the post.

## Instructions

1. Quickly look at the slot.
2. Push to the top of the crease.
3. Stop hard and face the face-off dot.
4. Rotate and use path of direction to move directly across to the other corner at the top of the crease.
5. Stop hard on your lead leg at the top corner of the crease in a set position and face the face-off dot.
6. Rotate and T-push to the short side post.
7. Stop in a set position on the post. Quickly glance at the back door.

## Coaching Tips

- Ensure you are in line with the face-off dot at each stop at the top of the crease.
- Use path of direction to move between points on the crease to continually cover the middle of the net.
- Move to each position by leading with your stick and head and carrying your hands in front of your body.

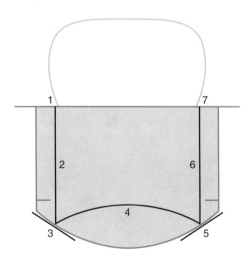

# Two-Stop Box With Butterfly Drill

## Purpose

In this drill, the goaltender works on far side and short side butterflies and recoveries.

## Setup

The goaltender starts in a set position at the post.

## Instructions

1. Quickly look to the slot using soft focus.
2. T-push to the top corner of the crease facing the face-off dot.
3. Drop down into a butterfly.
4. Recover, turn head and shoulders, step, rotate, and then T-push across the opposite top corner of the crease facing the face-off dot.
5. Drop down into a butterfly.
6. Rotate and T-push to the post.
7. End in a set position at the post. Quickly look to the back door.

## Coaching Tips

- When dropping down into the butterfly, it is important to go down with purpose as if you are making a save. Don't just drop down aimlessly.
- Carry out the drill in gamelike fashion. Maintain soft focus throughout the drill.

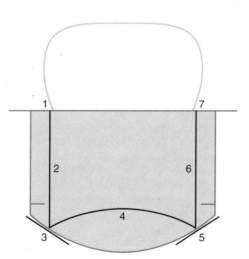

# Post and Out With Butterfly Drill

## Purpose

This drill requires the goaltender to focus on path of direction to get to the top of the crease. The goalie must pay close attention to dropping down in the butterfly with purpose and recovering to the post while maintaining proper form.

## Setup

The goaltender starts at the top of the crease in a regular stance.

## Instructions

1. Drop down into a butterfly.
2. Turn head and shoulders, rotate, and T-push to the post.
3. Set on the post and look in the slot, utilizing soft focus.
4. Push back to the top of the crease. Use path of direction to get back to the top of the paint. Drop down again into the butterfly.
5. Rotate and T-push to the opposite post.
6. Set position on post, utilizing soft focus.

## Coaching Tips

- Drive off the post leading with your head, keeping your hands out front, and driving with your stick to the top of the paint.
- Using path of direction, focus on coming through the middle of the crease.

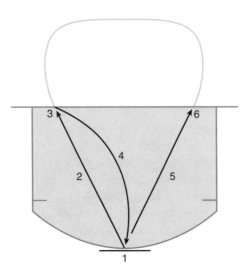

# Chapter 3
# Save Execution

Chapter 2 was about preparing to stop the puck. In it, we discussed various stances and the importance of leading all crease movements with your head and stick, having active hands, and putting yourself in optimal position to stop a shot. Chapter 2 also discussed path of direction and the importance of implementing both hard and soft focus into your game. We discussed how stance and movement are linked to your mental game—in essence, the attitude you bring to the ice. This chapter explores what to do when facing an actual shot. We touch on some foundational principles and discuss various types of saves. The chapter concludes with a series of drills designed to incorporate stance, movement, and proper save execution.

## FUNDAMENTALS OF MAKING A SAVE

It is important to remember that when executing a save, efficiency plays a key role in the process. The goaltender who incorporates the proper save selection is more likely to recover in position and be ready to face the next shot. Following are the key fundamentals involved in executing the save process with utmost efficiency and precision.

### Efficiency

Efficiency is a key component a goaltender must incorporate into his game to ensure he chooses the proper save selection. Efficiency is the ability to read a play using soft focus and always move straight into position. These two key factors separate successful goaltenders from the rest. Goaltenders who are efficient tend to see the game at a slower pace than those who are inefficiently, madly scrambling around in their crease looking for the puck. You must learn to slow down your game and use calculated, efficient movements, always ensuring you take the save process to completion.

## Save Execution

Mastering the basics and playing with proper positioning and controlled movements helps ensure that saves look simple and controlled. Although we all marvel at the "five-alarm" diving save, the reality is that this type of stop is often an indication that an error was made by the goaltender earlier in the save-execution process.

It is important to understand that a save is far more than stopping a shot. There are three phases to making a save: preparation, the save, and the post-save recovery.

1. *Preparation*. Good preparation involves reading the play and moving into optimal position in a strong stance.
2. *The save*. As the shot approaches, selecting the correct save execution and tracking the puck into and away from the body are key components of the save itself.
3. *Postsave recovery*. How you control the rebound and prepare for the next potential shot is of utmost importance. This requires a calm, controlled save execution and a technique that, whenever possible, leaves you balanced and in optimal position to move and face the next shot. This involves either clearing or covering the puck. In the case of a rebound, the save is not complete until you have recovered properly into position and are ready to execute the next save. Postsave recovery is covered in depth in chapter 4.

## Visual Attachment

Visual attachment is the ability when making a save to track a shot all the way into the body and all the way back out. Visual attachment applies regardless of where the puck is on the ice. Visual attachment does not apply only to shots on goal. In short, you should never take your eyes off the puck. Don't turn the shot aside and then look for the puck. Many goaltenders will see a shot coming and, after making the save, frantically try to find the puck. It is imperative that you see the puck in and then see it out. Both eyes are always looking squarely at or are "attached" to the puck.

# THE BUTTERFLY

Although there is a common belief that how fast a goaltender can get up reflects his effectiveness, the reverse is true. How fast you can drop down and be in a save position is the most important attribute you can have. If you can drop down quickly, you can stay on your feet longer and let the play come to you. When you stay on your feet as long as possible, you are less vulnerable in the top portion of the net. Goaltenders who are slow dropping into their butterfly must drop earlier to compensate for their lack of quickness. Dropping too early exposes the top portion of the net for a longer period.

Most saves are made from the butterfly position or a slight variation of it. There are two types of butterfly positions. The *active butterfly* is an upright position with active hands and is used for plays that are farther out (figure 3.1). The *blocking butterfly* is more compact, keeping everything tight, and is used for plays in close (figure 3.2).

Whichever form of the butterfly you choose to use is dependent on the play taking place in front of you. The techniques used to drop into the

Figure 3.1    Active butterfly.

Figure 3.2    Blocking butterfly.

butterfly and then move from that position are the same regardless of whether you are in a blocking or an active butterfly position.

# Dropping Into the Butterfly Position

When dropping into either variation of the butterfly position, it is important not to force your butterfly to be too wide. Let your position come to you naturally. When you use an unnatural butterfly and try to go as wide as you can, it slows you down as you go to the ice. So although the idea of a wide butterfly is that it gives you more coverage, in effect it is a slower movement than using a natural butterfly and therefore leaves more of the net exposed for a longer period.

Building on your butterfly width takes time and practice. It is much like a bodybuilder trying to build muscle mass on his arms. It takes time for muscles to grow, just as it takes time for a goaltender's flexibility to increase. Some believe that being as tall and straight as possible provides the most coverage in the butterfly. However, you should have a slight forward lean. Although you may appear smaller to the shooter, your angle to the puck provides more net coverage.

The steps for dropping into the butterfly position are as follows:

1. Starting in a ready position from the regular stance, drive your knees down to the ice. Let your hips generate the power to your knees as you go down.

2. When dropping into the butterfly, keep your feet in their set position on the ice. Although you are butterflying forward, only your knees should move ahead. Do not move your feet forward; they remain in a set position on the ice.

3. Have a slight bend at the waist, and stay agile with hands up in a ready position.

Note that there are still some goaltenders who utilize a narrow butterfly. Remember that any time you make your butterfly position abnormally wide or narrow, it slows down your movement and leaves portions of the net exposed for a longer period. It is always beneficial to drop into your butterfly using your natural hip flexibility.

---

**Goaltender Tips: Dropping Into the Butterfly**

- Be patient, staying on your feet as long as possible.
- Work on quickness rather than width.
- Know when to use a blocking butterfly and when to use an active butterfly.
- Have a slight forward lean at the waist.
- Keep pressure on your knees and seal them tight to the ice. Keep your elbows in and your hands in a ready position. The stick remains out front. Keep your head slightly forward.

# Moving in the Butterfly Position

Once in the butterfly position, there are three primary methods of moving within the crease: the inside-edge push, the back-leg recovery, and the butterfly slide.

## Inside-Edge Push

The inside-edge push is used to move across your crease when down in the butterfly position (figure 3.3). This is utilized when you want to end up in a butterfly position at a different destination in the crease.

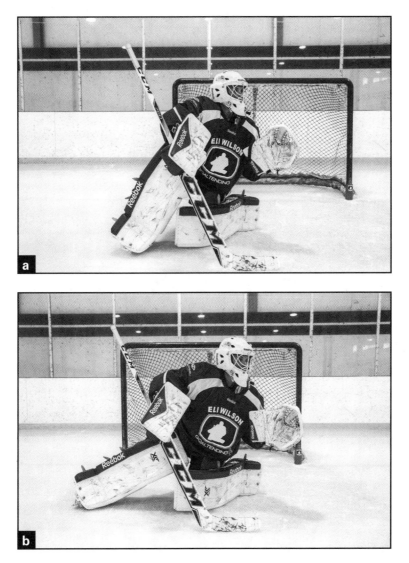

Figure 3.3   The goaltender *(a)* digs the inside edge of the skate into the ice and *(b)* pushes across.

The steps for the inside-edge push are as follows:

1. Before moving across, make sure your head and shoulders take a slight turn in the direction of your destination.
2. Plant the back skate on an angle toward your destination. Ensure that the inside edge of your skate blade is in contact with the ice.
3. Keep the lead shoulder and leg forward.
4. Push off and return to a butterfly at your destination.

### Goaltender Tips: Inside-Edge Push

- Ensure that you turn and move everything toward your destination, not away from it.
- Keep your hands in position as you arrive at your destination. Your lead hand always turns toward your destination, and your back hand follows. At one time, goalies would swing both their hands in the opposite direction they were moving in to try to gain momentum.
- Keep your head down, looking toward the puck.

## Back-Leg Recovery

Many times throughout a game, when down in the butterfly, the goaltender will be required to move to a new destination and end up on his feet in a stance. This is best attained by using the back-leg recovery, also known as a rotation recovery (figure 3.4).

The steps for the back-leg recovery are as follows:

1. Turn your head and shoulders in the direction you want to move.
2. Bring your front leg slightly underneath your body.
3. Maintain active hands throughout the movement.
4. Bring your back leg slightly behind, plant your skate on an angle, and drive off the back skate.
5. Open up the lead skate and T-push into position, returning to a regular stance.

### Goaltender Tips: Back-Leg Recovery

- Make sure the lead side of your body doesn't move away from the direction you wish to travel.
- Remember that "once it goes, it stays." Never move a part of your body one way and then pull back to load up. Do not pull your upper body in the opposite direction of your destination when trying to load power on your back leg. Simply move into position. Think of a sprinter. You won't see him lean back to get power on his back leg. When the gun sounds, he moves everything forward toward the finish line.
- Avoid jerky motions.

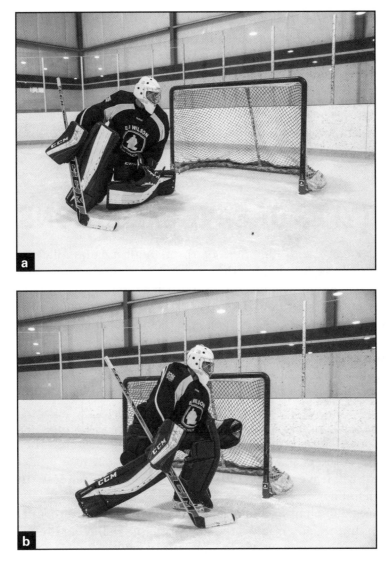

Figure 3.4    A goaltender *(a)* recovers from the butterfly position by driving off the back skate and *(b)* moves into position.

## Butterfly Slide

The butterfly slide is used when the goaltender is moving from a stance and sliding into a butterfly position at a new destination in the crease. The steps for the butterfly slide are as follows:

1. Start in a set position.
2. Turn your head; turn your shoulders.
3. Lead with the lead side of your body.

4. Turn and pivot with your lead leg.

5. Push off your back leg and land on your lead knee, sliding directly into position and ending up in a butterfly.

---

**Goaltender Tips: Butterfly Slide**

- Using soft focus, turn your head slightly to see the play around you.
- Do not pull your body away from your target destination.

# TYPES OF SAVE EXECUTIONS

A goaltender can spend long periods throughout a game following the play but not actually facing a shot. However, when that shot eventually comes, it's time to select and execute the proper save technique. It's not just about getting any part of your body to the puck to stop it from going in the net. It is important that you use the proper save technique applicable to the type of shot you are facing. If done correctly, you should find yourself in good position to stop a potential second shot.

## Glove Saves

At first thought, one may believe that a glove save is a simple technique—catch the puck! Yet so many goaltenders have not mastered this skill. The glove is one of the best ways to control rebounds because a puck that has been caught will leave no rebound. For this reason, we reiterate the concept of "active hands."

As discussed in chapter 2 on preparing for the shot, wherever the glove is held—high, midrange, or low—the key principle is having it out in front of your body, ready to make a save. Your finger position in the glove changes naturally whether catching a high or low shot. It is best to avoid thinking too much about where to hold your glove or how to position your fingers in the glove.

A glove save (figure 3.5) can be executed from both a standing and a butterfly position. Whenever going down, it is important to go down with a purpose, and while tracking, stay on top of the shot. Too many goaltenders have a reactionary drop-and-block habit where they first drop with hands low before reacting to the shot. At best, it causes a delay, as hands first drop and then must fight against momentum to move back up to catch the puck. At worst, it causes the goaltender to pull off and away from the puck, getting out of the way of the shot. From both positions, you must track the puck, stay on top of the shot, and watch it all the way into the glove, catching it in front of the body, not to the side. The steps for the glove save are as follows:

1. Watch the puck. Keep your eyes down on the puck all the way to see it into your glove.
2. Have your hand meet the puck. Do not catch pucks behind your body.
3. Accept the puck into the pocket of the glove. Once the puck hits the back of the glove pocket, close the glove.

## Goaltender Tips: Glove Save

- Using visual attachment, ensure both of your eyes are looking squarely at the puck.
- Make sure you can see your hands.
- Avoid "bobbling" the puck.

Figure 3.5    The goaltender *(a)* accepts the puck into the pocket of the glove and *(b)* closes it.

## Blocker Saves

While a glove save may seem routine to many, making a proper blocker save that controls the rebound by angling it into the corner can be significantly more challenging. To initialize proper blocker-hand positioning, the goalie should keep his wrist in a nearly straight line with his forearm. The key to executing a proper blocker save is to be able to direct the rebound into the corner (figure 3.6). While some goaltenders at the NHL level can direct shots off the blocker up ice and onto the stick of a teammate, we are going to focus on directing pucks into the corner.

The steps for the blocker save are as follows:

1. Keep your hands up in an active position.
2. Watch the puck all the way to your blocker.
3. Turn your wrist outward to direct the puck into the corner.
4. Using visual attachment, watch the puck off your blocker.
5. Control the angle of the face of the blocker up and down. On higher shots close to the body, there is a tendency to reach with the hand, which directs shots high and often dangerously out of control. The elbow must be held up so you do not direct pucks too high, causing unpredictable rebounds. How you angle your blocker is dependent on where the shot is positioned on the blocker side. You may want to direct the puck downward and into the corner or up and out of play. The key is that you want to control the rebound and angle it out of harm's way. Although not recommended, more-experienced goaltenders can direct the puck to a teammate up ice.

**Figure 3.6**   The goaltender watches the puck all the way into and off the blocker.

**Goaltender Tips: Blocker Save**

- Focus on your visual attachment.
- Do not move your body away from the shot.
- Do not let your hands drop before reacting to the puck.

# Stick Saves

Most shots along the ice can be easily stopped and controlled by the goaltender. With a strong butterfly technique and an active stick, shots can be readily deflected into the corner or out of play. A shot steered into the corner no longer poses an immediate threat, and a shot deflected out of play with the stick is the essence of rebound control. Playing the puck over the glass with the stick is just as effective as catching or trapping a puck.

As a rule, short side shots should not be handled with the stick. A short side shot that is ramped into the glass or off a stanchion will often create an unpredictable rebound that quickly pops above the goal line into a dangerous position. Short side shots along the ice can be better controlled with a butterfly pad save that keeps the puck on the ice while moving it below the goal line (butterfly pad saves are discussed later in this chapter).

## Defending Far Blocker-Side Shots

When defending a far blocker-side shot, you should deflect the puck out of play. Turn your stick off the thigh rise of the pad, and send the puck over the glass behind the net (figure 3.7).

Figure 3.7   When defending against the far-side blocker shot, the goaltender turns the stick off the thigh rise of his pad.

---

**Goaltender Tips: Far-Side Blocker Shots**

- Watch the puck all the way to and off your stick.
- Don't slice at the puck; let it come to the stick, and turn it aside by rotating the paddle of your stick off of your thigh rise. Aim to send it over the glass and out of play.

## Defending Far-Side Glove Shots

Defending the far-side glove shot requires a different technique than the one used on blocker-side shots. In this situation, keep your stick along the ice at an angle and use a knifing motion to send the puck into the corner or out of play (figure 3.8).

---

**Goaltender Tips: Far-Side Glove Shots**

- Do not change the angle of the stick blade and attack the shot, or you might direct the puck into the top corner of the net.
- Use visual attachment when executing the save.

**Figure 3.8** When defending against the far-side glove shot, the goaltender angles the stick and uses a knifing motion.

# Pad Saves

There are numerous occasions throughout a game when using the pads in the butterfly is the most efficient and effective way to stop the puck.

The pad save is an extension of the butterfly. The key to executing a proper pad save is to be able to extend the leg, making the save while keeping your other leg in position. Many goaltenders flare out both legs to make the save, putting themselves off balance and out of position for the next shot. A pad save is executed to one side or straight on.

## Pad Save to One Side

The steps for the pad save to one side are as follows.

1. From the butterfly position, with your knees firmly on the ice, extend the pad that will be making the save (figure 3.9).
2. Keep the pad firmly on the ice.
3. Use visual attachment to keep your eyes on the puck until after it hits the pad.

Figure 3.9    The goaltender in this pad save to one side has his pad firmly on the ice while watching the puck into and off the pad.

## Straight-On Pad Save

The steps to the straight-on pad save are as follows.

1. Keep your knees tight and compact and stop the puck in your pads (figure 3.10).
2. If you are unable to smother the rebound, use visual attachment to follow the puck into and off your pads.

Figure 3.10   The goaltender drops into the butterfly while keeping the knees tight and compact.

---

### Goaltending Tips: Pad Save

- Move only one side of your body. The pad making the save is extended while the other stays in position.
- Slightly transfer your weight toward the save leg to ensure the pad has a tight seal to the ice.
- Maintain control and coverage with the hands and upper body for both balance and coverage.
- Track the puck all the way into and away from the body, maintaining visual attachment as you bring your head through the motion of the save and rebound.
- Whenever you go down into the butterfly, go down with a purpose; don't just drop.

# Body-Containment Saves

All of us have seen players slam their sticks in frustration after hitting the goaltender right in the chest with a shot. The assumption is that the shooter executed a poor shot, but in reality, the goaltender stopped and controlled the shot through strong movement and positioning. A goaltender's taking a shot in the chest or the gut is often a sign of superior positioning and save selection. This scenario happens so often in a game that the goaltender should regularly practice body-containment saves (figure 3.11). The steps for a body-containment save are as follows:

1. The position of a body-containment save is a butterfly, with hands forward and tight to the body, ready to contain the puck. Do not allow the blocker to come in so far that it deflects the puck and causes a rebound.
2. Watch the puck all the way into your body.
3. Bend at the waist and keep your upper body as soft as possible.
4. Absorb and contain the puck into your upper body.
5. Collapse your body over the top of the puck.

Figure 3.11    The goaltender absorbs the shot into his upper body, supports the save with his glove, and collapses over the top of the puck to ensure containment.

**Goaltending Tips: Body-Containment Save**

- Keep your stick on the ice. Do not try to cover the puck in your body using your blocker hand. If the puck escapes your body, you will need to retrieve the puck with your stick.
- Support the save with the glove so the puck drops off the body into the glove. Bring the blocker across to contain the puck after it hits you.
- Be as soft as possible and absorb the puck into the body.

# SAVE-EXECUTION DRILLS

Goaltenders of all levels need to pay attention to detail. As the puck hits you, are you watching it all the way into and out of your body? Do you always have active hands, or do you let them drop as you become tired? When you butterfly, are you driving your knees to the ice with purpose, or are you just letting yourself drop down? When you make glove saves, are you watching the puck into the pocket of the glove? Do you consciously direct blocker shots into the corner, or do you just let the puck hit you and then try to find it? Do you always aim to fully contain body shots, or do you just let the puck bounce off you?

The following drills are a progression of everything we have learned so far. Starting with glove and blocker saves, we progress through stick, pad, and body-containment saves. Remember that all the drills incorporate stance and movement, so pay attention to details and perform every drill with purpose. Whether it be working on glove saves specifically or any other component of the position, goaltenders should always train with purpose. Think of the golfer who goes to a driving range and indiscriminately smashes golf balls as far as he can. This will have very little effect on improving his golf game. Instead, what if he were to work with different clubs at different times and focus on one or two specific areas of improvement? Do you think this technique would improve his game? It's the same for the goaltender. For every drill you perform, have a purpose in mind and strive toward continuous improvement.

# Moving-Glove Drill

## Purpose

In a game, pucks get shot and deflected both high and low, and you will rarely have time to consciously set your glove in an optimal position. Instead, you need to develop a more reactive glove. This exercise is designed to reinforce the ability to react to pucks in a variety of situations, catching pucks high when the glove is low and low when the glove is high, regardless of how the glove may be moving. This is a slightly abstract exercise, but it provides great results.

a

## Setup

The goaltender assumes a basic stance midcrease.

## Instructions

1. The goaltender starts to move his glove into random positions—down *(a)*, up *(b)*, in, and *(c)* out.

2. While the goaltender is moving the glove, a shooter shoots random pucks to the glove side.

b

c

# Hold-Glove Save

## Purpose

In this drill, the goaltender works on making alternate glove and blocker saves while building muscle memory and proper form and technique.

## Setup

The goaltender starts midcrease in a butterfly position. The shooter is positioned in the high slot.

## Instructions

1. The shooter takes shots alternating between the glove and blocker.
2. React to the shot on the glove or blocker side.
3. Turn your head into the shot.
4. If the shot is on the blocker side, turn the blocker out and direct the puck to the near-side corner. If the shot is on the glove side, catch the puck in the pocket of the glove.
5. Hold the save position for two seconds.

## Coaching Tips

- Always start in and revert to the correct ready position before each shot.
- Use visual attachment.
- Do not move away from the shot.

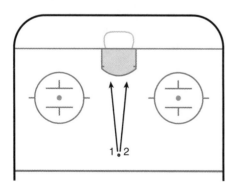

# Mirror Save

## Purpose

This drill allows the goaltender to work on glove and blocker saves, focusing on proper form on both the glove and blocker sides. Mirror saves can be used with almost any type of save. They are designed to train the nervous system by beginning with the end in mind. The goaltender works backward to drill in the correct form before executing the save.

## Setup

The goaltender starts midcrease in a butterfly save position. One shooter is placed in the high slot.

## Instructions

1. The shooter takes shots between the goaltender's glove and the blocker.
2. Rewind from the save position back into a regular butterfly.
3. As the shot approaches, revert into the butterfly save position to stop the shot.
4. If the shot is on the blocker side, the goaltender turns the blocker out and direct the puck to the near-side corner. If the shot is on the glove side, catch the shot in the pocket of the glove.

## Coaching Tips

- Perform the movements precisely and slowly. Do not rush the drill.
- Use proper form in the mirror save.
- Rewind back into the butterfly slowly before facing the shot.

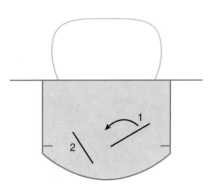

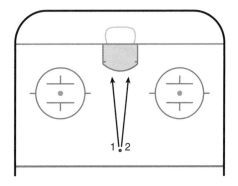

# Post and Out for Shot Drill

## Purpose

This drill allows the goaltender to work on stick saves while incorporating path of direction, soft focus, bringing the head through the motion of the save, and postsave recovery.

## Setup

The goaltender sets at the top of the paint ready to face a shot. A shooter is set up in the high slot in the center.

## Instructions

1. The goaltender turns the head, then the shoulders, and rotates. Using the T-push, he pushes directly to the post.
2. The goaltender stops in a set post stance. Using soft focus, he quickly looks to the slot.
3. Using path of direction, the goaltender pushes back to the top of the crease.

4. The shooter shoots hard along the ice, low to the opposite post from which the goaltender comes.
5. The goaltender executes the stick save.
6. The goaltender follows the rebound.
7. Repeat the drill with the goalie going to the opposite post.

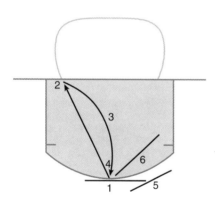

## Coaching Tips

- When making the stick save, don't just lazily drop in the butterfly to make the save.
- Keep both hands active.
- Turn your head and shoulders into the shot.
- Keep your stick flat on the ice and turn the shot to the corner, deflecting it off the glass or into the boards.
- Maintain visual attachment. See the shot into and off your stick.
- Follow the rebound as hard as you can.

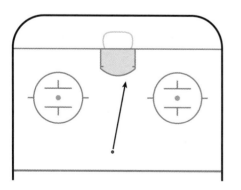

# Side-to-Side Shots Drill

## Purpose

This drill allows the goaltender to work on stick saves; back-leg recovery; and quick, explosive movements.

## Setup

Two shooters are at the top of each face-off circle, each with a puck. The goaltender starts at the top of his crease, facing one of the shooters.

## Instructions

1. The goaltender pushes across and sets.
2. One shooter shoots hard and low to the far side of the goaltender.
3. The goaltender drops into a butterfly, makes the stick save, and turns the puck to the corner.
4. The goaltender rotates and using path of direction, T-pushes across the crease to the other side.
5. The goaltender now faces the other shooter, drops down to make the save with his stick, controls the puck, locates the next puck, and pushes across into position to face the first shooter.

## Coaching Tips

- Use visual attachment to see puck in and out.
- Do a maximum of six repetitions.
- Keep the drill under control. Keep up a fast pace without sacrificing technique.

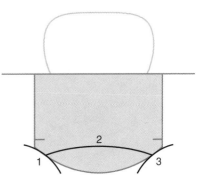

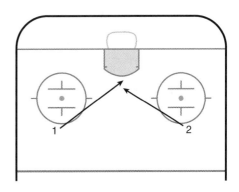

# Single-Shot Patience Drill

## Purpose

This drill is intended to work on the goaltender's ability to remain patient when going down in the butterfly to make a save. This drill also develops the goaltender's hands and his ability to read the shooter while always maintaining visual attachment with the puck.

## Setup

The goaltender is positioned at the top of his crease in a regular stance. Two more goaltenders are positioned at the hash marks. A shooter is stationed just inside the blue line.

## Instructions

1. The shooter takes a shot to either the glove or blocker side.
2. The goaltenders stationed at the hash marks drop into a butterfly.
3. Only after the two goaltenders at the hash marks have dropped into the butterfly can the goalie in the crease drop down to make the save.

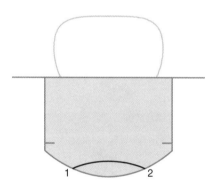

## Coaching Tips

- Be patient. Be sure to wait for the puck to pass the two goalies stationed at the hash marks before dropping down to make the save.

- If this drill is performed in a team practice where there are only two goalies available, simply place only one goalie at the hash marks.

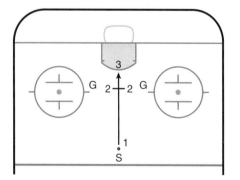

# Far-Side Stick Save With Second-Shot Drill

## Purpose

This drill allows the goalie to work on far-side shots, stick saves, rebound control, back-leg recoveries, and body-containment saves.

## Setup

The goaltender starts at his post in a set position. Three shooters are needed for this drill. Shooter A is placed with a puck at the hash mark by the wall. Shooters B and C are placed outside of opposite face-off circles. Shooter C has a puck.

## Instructions

1. The goaltender T-pushes to the top of the crease and drops into a butterfly position.
2. Shooter A passes the puck to shooter B, and shooter B takes a shot to the far side of the goaltender.
3. The goaltender makes a stick save, recovers, rotates, and T-pushes to the other side of the crease.
4. Once on the other side of the crease, the goaltender drops into a butterfly position, and shooter C then shoots hard to score.
5. The goaltender stops the shot from shooter C and then follows the rebound.

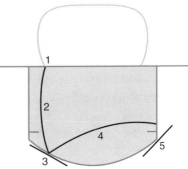

## Coaching Tips

- Stay balanced.
- Do not move out of position to "load up" when moving across.
- Pay attention to all details.
- Try to put the first shot over the glass and out of play.
- Try to cover all loose pucks.

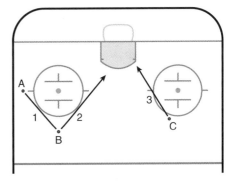

# Double Pass, Double Shot Drill

## Purpose

This drill allows the goalie to work on beating the pass and low far-side shots, controlling rebounds, and getting into position to face a second shot. Because the last shot in this drill is a shoot-to-score, the goaltender must be ready to make any type of save while controlling and containing the puck.

## Setup

The goaltender starts at the post in a set position. Three shooters are required for this drill. Shooter A is placed with a puck at the near-side hash mark. Shooter B is positioned outside of the face-off circle. Shooter C is positioned with a second puck outside of the opposite face-off circle.

## Instructions

1. Shooter A passes to shooter B, and at the same time, the goaltender moves to the top of the crease, facing shooter B.

2. Shooter B passes to shooter C, and at the same time, the goaltender turns, rotates, and T-pushes to the opposite side of the crease, beating the pass.

3. Shooter C passes the puck back to shooter B, and at the same time, the goaltender turns, rotates, and T-pushes back across the crease, beating the pass.

4. Shooter B shoots far side on the goalie while the goaltender drops into a butterfly and makes a stick save on shooter B.

5. The goaltender turns, rotates, and T-pushes across the crease to face a shot from shooter C.

6. Shooter C then shoots to score, and the goaltender stops and contains the puck.

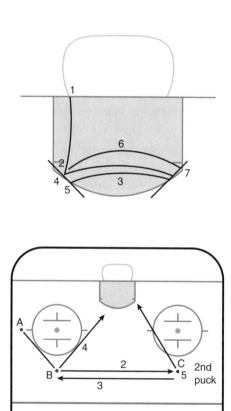

## Coaching Tips

- Remain competitive when performing this drill.
- Stay over the puck when making the stick save. Don't pull back in the wrong direction while making the save.
- Use soft focus and visual attachment.
- Make sure the first save is performed to completion.
- Pay attention to all details.
- Perform drill as gamelike as possible.

# Double Lateral Pass and Shot Drill

## Purpose

The purpose of this drill is for the goaltender to work on beating the pass in both directions, using soft focus, and containing the puck.

## Setup

The goaltender starts at his post in a set position (G1). Three shooters are needed for this drill. Shooter A is placed with a puck at the hash mark by the wall. Shooters B and C are placed outside of opposite face-off circles.

## Instructions

1. Shooter A passes the puck to shooter B, and at the same time, the goaltender T-pushes to the top of the crease and gets in a set position (G2).
2. Shooter B passes the puck to shooter C, and at the same time, the goaltender T-pushes across the crease and gets into a set position (G3).
3. Shooter C immediately passes the puck back to shooter B while the goaltender T-pushes back across the crease and gets into a set position (G4). Shooter B takes a shot on goal, and the goaltender drops into a butterfly to make the save (G5).

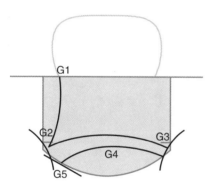

## Coaching Tips

- Don't cheat the pass; beat the pass!
- Stay square and push.
- Follow rebounds.
- Cover loose pucks.

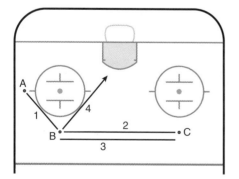

# Chapter 4

# Postsave Recovery

Chapter 3 was about save execution. We discussed the importance of visual attachment, always staying focused on the puck, and watching shots all the way into and off you. We looked at various butterfly movements and how to best navigate your crease using inside-edge pushes, back-leg recoveries, and butterfly slides. We focused on pad, glove, stick, and body saves. However, there is more to the save process after the puck contacts you.

The ability to control rebounds and get into position and make second and third saves is one of the key components that separates goaltenders at all levels. This chapter focuses on what to do after you have made the first save. Where do you direct the puck? How do you set up for further play? Do you stay up or down? We look at different types of rebounds and talk about the strategy to best prepare yourself for a second and third shot. We also introduce lead-leg recoveries, which allow you to move off the post and prepare for the next shot with more speed and efficiency than ever. We discuss the difference between post leans and post reaches. The chapter concludes with gamelike simulation drills that require you to navigate throughout your crease, stop multiple shots, and direct rebounds with complete control and efficiency.

## POSTSAVE RECOVERY SKILLS

Postsave recovery is your ability to track rebounds by following the puck, gauging what you want to do next, and setting up for a second shot. It is important to stay focused, in position, and not move away from the puck. Once the puck hits you, watch it to see where you need to move next. When moving to your next spot, you want to fill the space in the middle of the net as quickly as possible. After making the save, you need to gauge how much time you have before the next shot. You should ask yourself, "Is there time to get up and move to the next position, or am I going to stay down?" You can either move into a new position or stay in your current position if the rebound is in close or the shooter is close to the puck.

There is an element of intuition in choosing whether to get up or stay down to face the next shot. It is dependent on timing. If the rebound comes out to a shooter who is in close, you will want to move using path of direction, keeping your body tight (blocking butterfly) to face the second shot. If the rebound goes out a little farther but the shooter is still close to the puck, you will still want to stay down and use a butterfly with active hands to make the save. On the other hand, if the shot goes out to a shooter at a farther distance and the shooter is a little farther away from the puck, you will have more time before the shot is released. In those situations, you should get to your feet and move into position to face the second shot.

You may think that if the rebound is far out, you can get up on your feet, whereas if the rebound is nearby, you should stay down. However, that decision is based on the puck's location in relation to the opposing players. Your decision to stay up or go down depends on the player's proximity to the puck. If the shooter is close to the puck, stay down. If the shooter is farther away from the puck, then it is better to get up and ready yourself for the next shot. In case of a tie where it appears you may have time to get up but are uncertain, the safer bet is to stay down and cover the higher-risk play by blocking the lower part of the net. If the rebound goes out to the side, with the potential of another shot coming immediately, you have to load with your inside edge and outside skate to push across and explode into a save. By explode, we mean moving quickly and powerfully. It is always easier to move across in a down position and then get up than to start moving on your feet and then have to drop down midway through your movement.

After making a first save, push into position with the intent of filling the middle of the net as quickly as possible and analyzing the risk of a second shot. If there is no imminent risk of a second shot, you can stand up onto your feet and into position by using a rotation recovery T-push. Whether staying down or standing up, always be aware of the path of direction in your movements.

## Extinction of the Vertical Horizontal and the Reverse Vertical Horizontal

Before we begin our discussion on defending the post on plays that come from behind the net or out of the corners, let's talk a little about two very popular post stances used in the goaltending community: the vertical horizontal (VH) and the reverse VH. These terms are needlessly complex and outdated. Since the premise of this book is to simplify the goaltending position, we are replacing the VH with blocker-side and glove-side post leans. The reverse VH will be referred to as a lean. Shoulder lean positions are used to defend against plays out of the corner, including pass plays, sharp-angle shots, and wraparounds, which are discussed in more detail later in the book.

We assume that you have heard the terms VH and reverse VH. In this book, our goal is to simplify the goaltender position and the terminology that goalies use, so we oppose confusing terms such as these. The VH moniker was coined at a time when coaches were attempting to find scientific solutions to improve goaltending. What was originally called the knee drop evolved into the more technical-sounding vertical horizontal. The VH is a post position in which a goaltender drops down with his post pad up vertically and his other pad along the ice horizontally. Over time, this technique has proven to be cumbersome and ineffective for the following reasons:

- On low shots, the goaltender is not able to see the puck at his feet, so he has no visual attachment to the puck.
- It is extremely difficult to control rebounds in part because of the positioning of the vertical pad and the lack of eye contact the goaltender has on the puck.
- It is easy for opposition players to shoot at the horizontal pad, leaving the goaltender in an extremely vulnerable position for the rebound.
- It is very difficult for the goaltender to move from the VH position and recover pucks efficiently.
- The top short side of the net is completely exposed.

A far more effective position to take on the post is a lean position, which we discuss in this chapter. (Some call the post lean a reverse VH, another technical-sounding term that we avoid.) The post lean allows you to maintain far greater net coverage and see the puck even when it is at your feet.

# Post Position

When the puck is in the corner, you need to get a read on the developing play. If the risk level is low and you are not feeling pressure, you can stay on your feet at the post. As the play gets closer to the net, you will feel more pressure and may want to get into a ready position, which in this case is a lean against the post. When the play goes behind the net, rather than pushing hard post to post and overcommitting, a post reach is used to give you time, allowing you to use a detailed, patient system of defense when the puck is in high-risk areas.

## Post Leans

Many times rebounds are directed into the corner by the goaltender, and a post lean is required to defend the play from the corner. In contrast to the knee drop or VH, the post lean—on either the blocker or glove side—enables you to have both pads down on the ice in position for easy mobility and visual attachment to the puck. A shot that might hit you in the upper part of the pad using the knee drop will now hit you in the chest, and if a rebound is given off, you can drop down to cover it. Any puck that hits you in the pads will leave a rebound you can follow, allowing you to make a second save. You can see the puck no matter where it hits you, whereas in the knee drop, you can't. Further advantages to the blocker- or glove-side lean include the following:

- A shoulder lean allows you to move from post to post on your knees.
- Everything down low to the net is covered.
- Your hands are low to the ice, which allows you to access and cover pucks.

To execute the blocker-side lean, keep your pads tightly sealed along the ice, using your back leg for support, and keep your chest and hands up in an active ready position (figure 4.1). Feel the post against your shoulder. Keep a strong seal against the post, and don't overplay the situation and go beyond the post in your lean. If you get into a battle situation on the blocker side, you can defend it by using the paddle-down technique, which is covered later in this chapter.

Figure 4.1   Blocker-side lean.

The glove-side lean (figure 4.2) looks very much like the blocker-side lean. However, there are some differences in the way you defend on the glove side. Key things to note when executing the glove-side lean are as follows:

- Don't pull off the post early because it will leave you vulnerable to the short side.
- You may think you have the post tightly sealed, so the tendency is to stop watching the puck on the expectation that it will hit you. Always keep your eye on the puck.

Also, note that several times throughout this book we refer to back-leg recoveries, which are used to recover from a butterfly position and get up onto your feet. Lead-leg recoveries are used when you need to recover onto your feet from a post lean. Instead of driving off your back leg, you are using your lead leg to pull you up and into position on your feet. A back-leg recovery is used to move while staying down on the ice or moving onto your feet from the butterfly. You always recover with your back leg. When you are against the post, however, your lead-leg knee is already off the ice, so you simply pull yourself forward with the lead leg. Lead-leg recovery off the post allows you to move in one fluid motion. You cannot recover off your back leg when it is butted up against the post.

Figure 4.2    Glove-side lean.

To execute a lead-leg recovery, do the following:

- Point your lead skate in the direction you want to move.
- Open your front-leg skate in a C-cut position.
- Putting your weight on your front leg, pull yourself forward with your upper body using your chest, hands, and stick for momentum.
- Bring your head forward through the motion.

## Post Reaches

Now that we have studied the lean and how to best recover from that position to face a second shot, we are going to look at how to best follow the play and move post to post when the puck is behind the net. An opposition player skating back and forth behind the net can leave you in a precarious position. Which side will the opponent come from? Will he pass the puck out from behind the net? If so, from what side will the pass come? How do you as the goaltender follow the puck behind the net and still manage to track what is happening in front of the goal? In this section, we discuss post reaches. Post reaches allow you to reach your body across the net rather than slide post to post with little to no control.

Post reaches allow you to cover both posts so you won't be beaten on either side. If you push from post to post rather than reach, the shooter simply needs to get you moving in one direction and then go the opposite direction. On a reach, however, you can watch the puck and the shooter the whole time.

Because there are no absolutes in hockey, sometimes you must play based on feel. We try to eliminate the guessing game as much as possible by discussing positioning that will give you the best opportunity for success. In no other part of the game are you exposed to as many threats as when the puck is being played behind the net. For this reason, we have developed the 75-25 rule.

As you move side to side to defend the play behind the net, 75-25 refers to your commitment to either post. When a shooter is moving behind the net and you are in a lean position, you will be 100 percent committed to the near post. As the puck goes farther behind the net, you need to widen your stance, thus creating a window over your shoulder whereby you can see where the puck is. So as your stance widens, you are now committed 75 percent to the near post, but with 25 percent awareness and commitment to the far post (figure 4.3a). When the puck travels past the halfway point behind the net, you should move your upper body, keep your eyes on the puck, and commit 100 percent to the other post (figure 4.3b). As you move across, continue to watch the puck, and reach for the far post with your toe. Always bring your lower body across first and be in a ready position if the play should revert to the near-side post. This is one situation where you do not lead with your head to get to the other post. You want to keep your eye on the puck the whole time and then bring your head through the motion. Once the play moves out in front of the net, use a lead-leg recovery and move out to defend the play.

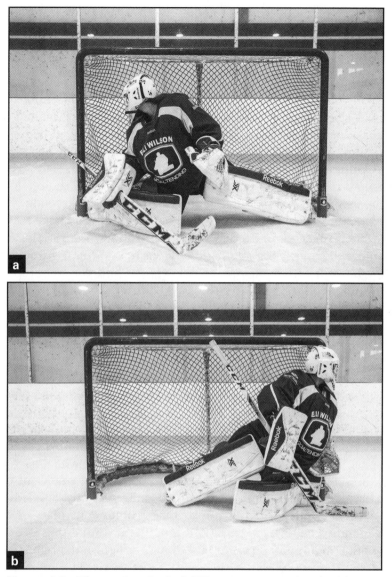

**Figure 4.3**  The goaltender is *(a)* 75 percent committed to his near post as he *(b)* begins to reach for the far post with his toe and commits 100 percent to the opposite post.

As the play is developing behind the net, there are situations developing in front of the goal. How do you watch both simultaneously? Soft focus, which was introduced in chapter 2, is used when the goaltender glances to see whether there are opposition players away from where the play is taking place. Active soft focus occurs when there is a shooter on the far side. So as you keep your eye on the puck behind the net, you must also use active soft focus to know where the open opposition shooter is out front. This way you can react to the play out front immediately after the puck has been passed from behind the net.

## Wraparounds

Many times, opposition players will try to wrap around from behind the net, catching you off guard. One of the most infamous wraparound clips from the NHL was Doug Gilmour's 1993 double overtime winner against St. Louis Blues goaltender Curtis Joseph. On the play, Gilmour moved back and forth behind the net. As Joseph tried to look over his shoulder, he lost sight of the puck, and Gilmour jammed it in past a sprawling Joseph. Had Joseph used post leans and reaches, he would have been able to track the puck and stop the shot by using the paddle-down technique on the blocker side.

When defending the wraparound to the blocker side, you have two options: Once the shooter has committed to wrapping around to the stick side (figure 4.4a), you can defend using the paddle-down technique (figure 4.4b). This should provide you with good coverage down low, and you will stop the puck with your stick and cover up any rebound. Rather than having the blade of your stick on the ice, put your paddle on the ice for low coverage. Because the paddle of the stick is much longer than the blade, you get more coverage.

You can use an active stick defense and attempt to take the puck off the opposition's stick (figure 4.5). The active-stick technique also allows you to keep your shoulder up higher, thereby defending the near-side top part of the net. The active-stick technique is better suited to breaking up pass plays out of the corner. Much like your hands, feet, and head, your stick is also an extremity, and it is important to focus on your stick as you move throughout the crease. Your stick guides you in so many movements, whether they be recoveries or T-pushes. Your stick acts as your steering wheel as you move. On a low far-side shot, activate your stick to deflect the puck out of harm's way or to break up a pass coming from the corner. An active stick allows you to corral and cover pucks, giving you better rebound control.

When defending a glove-side wraparound, it is essential that your glove be facing the puck in a ready position and that you maintain a tight seal on the post while continuing to watch the puck (figure 4.6). The most dangerous thing you can do is stop watching the puck because you assume you have a tight seal and the puck will just hit you. Developing plays can change in an instant, so it is imperative to never lose sight of the puck.

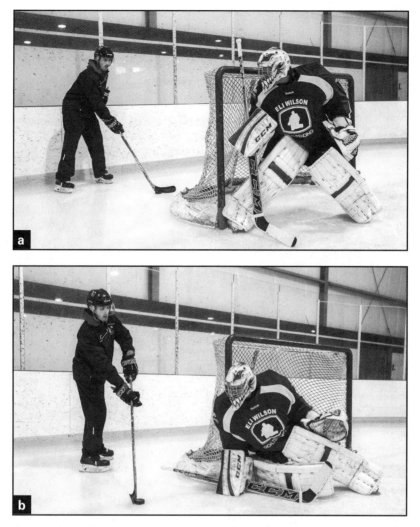

Figure 4.4 A goaltender *(a)* determines the shooter is wrapping around stick side, and *(b)* defends the wraparound with the paddle-down technique.

Figure 4.5 A goaltender defends with an active stick to intercept potential passes from the corner.

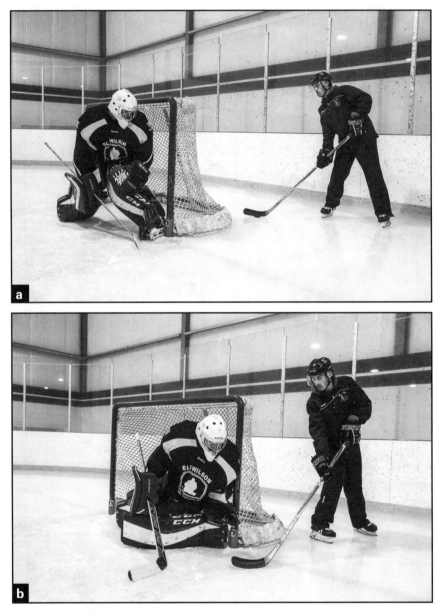

Figure 4.6  A goaltender defends *(a)* the glove-side wraparound with a tight seal to the post, and *(b)* seals the post and follows the puck with the glove in a ready position.

# Stretch Saves

There are instances when a rebound ends up in a dangerous position. Although you may be required to make a stretch save, you still want to be in control of your movements. The following are situations that can arise after making an initial save in a butterfly position. When the rebound goes to an opponent in close proximity to the net, you will need to first inside-edge push and then extend your body to make the save. You may be required to do one of the following:

## Inside-Edge Push Into an Extension

Assume that after making an initial save in a butterfly position, the rebound goes out to a dangerous spot, and the opposition shooter takes a high shot. You may be forced to inside-edge push and extend your upper body as far as possible to make the save (figure 4.7). You are in essence making a save while in motion. If the puck is not going to hit you while performing the inside-edge push, you have to extend your body to make the save. Since there are countless variables as to where the shooter is going to place the shot, the key is to inside-edge push and react to wherever the puck is headed. For example, you could be moving to your right, and the puck is shot to your left, forcing you to extend your body in the other direction.

## Inside-Edge Push Into a Full Split

In the case where a rebound goes to a shooter who quickly fires a shot to the low corner of the net, you may be required to extend your lower body into a full-split save position (figure 4.8). Any shot that cannot be stopped using a simple save is an extension of that simple save. The preceding play may have required you to move out of the center of your net. A shot approaches that is out of reach, and you are required to go into an extension to stop the puck.

## Inside-Edge Push Into Upper and Lower Extension

In other circumstances, you may be required to extend both your upper and lower body at the same time (figure 4.9). When you find yourself out of position and no longer in the middle of the net due to the previous play, you may be required to extend your body and reach farther than normal to make the save. If you were in perfect position to begin with, you would have to move only a few inches to make the save. When you are not in an ideal position to start with, you will have to extend your body to make what otherwise would have been a routine save. However, it is important to always stay in complete control of your movements even when facing a potential stretch save.

Figure 4.7   Upper-body extension.

Figure 4.8   Full split.

Figure 4.9   Upper-and lower-body extension.

# Net Management

Since a lot of this chapter focuses on the goaltender's moving laterally post to post, it is important that you move with precision between your posts. This is what we call net management. Net management is about not pushing outside the confines of your posts. In simple terms, it is the ability to move from post to post without pushing sideways beyond your post. How often have you seen a forward break down the wing on a goaltender who overplays the angle and has part of his body covering the outside portion of the net, leaving himself completely exposed on the far side? The key to net management is to be able to position yourself so that your body is always filling space in the net. Remember, any part of your body that is covering the outside portion of the net is wasted coverage because pucks cannot go in through the side of the net. Make sure you are always covering the 4 × 6 opening of the net.

There are situations where you are forced to play a little outside the confines of your post. For instance, if an opponent has the puck on the wall at the hash marks, you start on the post. As the shooter skates toward you with the puck, you need to do the following:

- Come off the post, at the shooter.
- Push out and overcover on the short-side post (figure 4.10a); otherwise, as soon as you drop into the butterfly, you will be exposed on the short side. Overcoverage means you are covering an area outside of the opening of the net. You cover that area down low because when you are facing a play from a sharp angle and you drop into a butterfly, your body goes straight down. Because of the angle, you actually pull out of the middle of the net. So if you overcover to the side, when you drop into the butterfly, you will be in the center of the net.
- By slightly overplaying the near-side post, when you drop into the butterfly, you will obtain full coverage of the net (figure 4.10b).

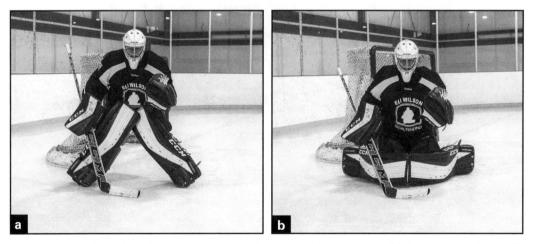

**Figure 4.10**    A goaltender (a) overcovers the near-side post and (b) drops into a butterfly with perfect net coverage.

# CORRALLING AND COVERING REBOUNDS

Covering pucks is an important skill that every goaltender needs in his repertoire. It may seem like a simple thing, but there are some crucial things that every goaltender needs to practice to retrieve and cover rebounds.

In many instances, a rebound will come off your upper body or pads and end up right in front of you. In this scenario, you want to retrieve the puck with your stick, pull it in, and cover it with your glove. Don't wait for the puck to get too far away from you; otherwise, you will be lunging at it, perhaps missing the puck altogether, leaving you on your stomach, out of position, and without the puck. Then, in one motion, reach around and grab the front of the puck with the back of the toe of your stick and pull it toward you; then cover it hard with your glove. When covering a puck, the idea is to attack the loose puck. Move your hand in a straight line to the puck, and cover it by putting your glove down on the ice hard, making sure you have the puck (figure 4.11).

Here are some additional points about covering:

- If you get into a situation where you are forced to make a paddle-down save, the puck will basically be "attached" to your paddle. Just reach over top of the paddle and cover the puck with your glove (figure 4.12).

**Figure 4.11** The goaltender retrieves the puck with the stick and covers it with the glove.

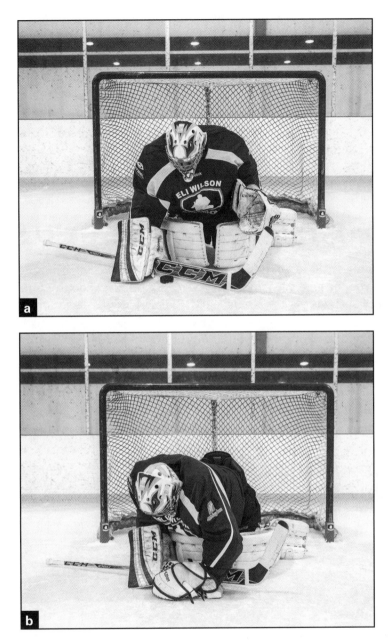

Figure 4.12 Paddle-down save: *(a)* The goaltender stops the puck using the paddle down technique, and *(b)* reaches over the top of the paddle and covers the puck with his glove.

- There are times when you are faced with a weak shot, and you will try to cover the puck in one motion as it comes to you. This can be a very risky approach because the puck can easily slip through an opening and into the net. Instead, it is imperative to stop the puck first and then cover it.
- If the rebound is just out of reach and it turns into an in-tight breakaway situation, always try to get to your feet to defend. Breakaways are discussed in more detail in chapter 6.
- If you are covering a puck that you never saved and it is loose in front of you, bring your glove down hard on the puck to ensure you cover it.

# POSTSAVE RECOVERY DRILLS

The following drills incorporate everything discussed in this chapter: post leans and reaches, active soft focus, covering pucks, second and third shots, and behind-the-net play. Many of the drills have gray areas built in to accommodate different kinds of rebounds. Pay close attention to detail and perform every drill as if it were a gamelike situation. It is very important when developing goaltenders to not make the drills static. Instead, you need to have structure, guidelines, and detail, but you do not want to be overly technical. Drills need to have gray areas because there are a variety of situations that can occur in a game.

# Reverse Rebound Drill

## Purpose

The purpose of this drill is to allow the goaltender to practice corralling pucks with the stick and covering them efficiently with the glove.

## Setup

Goaltender is in a butterfly position in front of the crease. A shooter is stationed on each side of the goaltender.

## Instructions

1. The shooters alternate shooting pucks off the goaltender's pads. When the puck hits the goaltender's pad, the puck will come out front.
2. The goaltender corrals the puck with his stick and covers it with the glove.
3. The goaltender clears the puck to the side and readies himself for the next shot.

## Coaching Tips

- The puck should be covered with purpose each time. Once covered, the puck should be pushed off to the side and ready for the next shot.

- Increase the challenge by stationing a coach behind the goaltender. The coach passes the puck out to the shooter, who directs a shot off the goaltender's pads. Since the goaltender is unaware of which side the puck will be passed from, he must stay alert and ready throughout the drill.

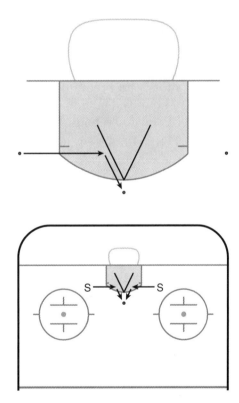

# Down and Up Shot Drill

## Purpose

The purpose of this drill is to allow the goaltender to work on different aspects of postsave recoveries, including soft and hard focus, post positioning, rotation recovery T-pushes, butterflies, inside-edge pushes, leans, and far-side stick saves.

## Setup

The goaltender starts at his post facing shooter A, who is stationed at the half wall with a puck. Shooter B is on the goal line beside the net, and shooter C is stationed at the top of the face-off circle.

## Instructions

1. Shooter A starts at the half wall and passes the puck down to shooter B, and shooter B passes the puck to shooter C. At the same time, the goaltender pushes out to the top corner of the crease to face shooter C.

2. Shooter C attempts to draw a rebound by shooting the puck low on either the short or the far side.

3. The goaltender stops the puck and follows the rebound. On short-side shots, the rebound will usually end up in the corner SSR (short-side rebound). On far-side shots, rebounds will generally be directed to R1, R2, or R3 (rebound positions 1, 2, and 3).

4. The goaltender then pushes across the crease to follow the rebound. If the rebound goes to position R1, the goaltender will rotate and T-push to the post. If the rebound goes to position R2, the goaltender will inside-edge push and follow the rebound. If it goes to position R3, the goaltender will recover, rotate, and T-push across the crease to follow the rebound.

# Coaching Tips

- Beat the pass by getting to the top of the crease with speed.
- Make all movements continuous and fluid. Pay attention to details by moving with your head first and without pulling out of position to load up.
- If the shot goes short side and the rebound travels into the corner, inside-edge push back to the post and into a lean position.
- Always be prepared for a high-risk situation by following the rebound in its entirety and finishing movements with attention to detail and soft focus.

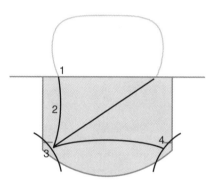

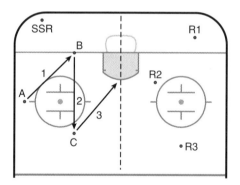

# Down and Up With a Second Shot

## Purpose

This drill allows the goaltender to work on making a short-side save without activating the stick and using the pad only. The goaltender has the choice whether to stay up at the post or go down. Active soft focus comes into play as the goaltender is looking for shooter D on the far side.

## Setup

The goaltender starts in a set position on the post. Four shooters are required for this drill. Shooter A is positioned at the half wall with a puck. Shooter B is on the goal line beside the net. Shooter C is stationed at the top of the face-off circle, and shooter D is positioned just inside the blue line on the opposite side.

## Instructions

1. The goaltender starts at the post (G1). Shooter A passes to shooter B at the goal line.
2. Shooter B passes the puck to shooter C at the top of the face-off circle. At the same time, the goaltender pushes out to the top of the crease (G2).
3. Shooter C takes a low, short-side shot on the goaltender. The goaltender makes the pad save on the low, short-side shot, steers the puck into the corner (G3), and then recovers, rotates, and pushes back to the post (G4) before pushing out to the top of the crease again (G5).
4. At the same time, shooter B skates to the corner, picks up a second puck, and passes it out to shooter D.
5. Shooter D shoots with the intent to score on the goaltender. The goaltender makes the save and, if the puck remains in play, follows the rebound (G6).

## Coaching Tips

- Decide whether to use the stick on the short side shot or just the pad. On a hard shot, avoid using the stick so you do not to give up an unpredictable rebound.
- Focus on moving to the short-side post in a fluid motion, getting your toe to the post.
- Use soft focus to maintain awareness of the second shooter.
- Be sure to beat the pass to the second shooter.

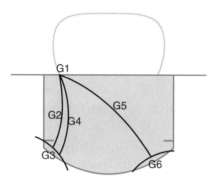

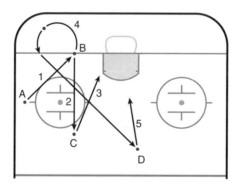

# Up, Across, and Back With a Second Shot

## Purpose

This drill incorporates all the skills necessary to perform the previous two drills. Additionally, this drill allows the goaltender to work on facing a second shot off a rebound utilizing an inside-edge push.

## Setup

The goaltender starts in a set position at the post. Three shooters are required. Shooter A is positioned at the half wall with a puck. Shooter B is situated on the outside of the near face-off circle. Shooter C is positioned with a second puck outside the opposite face-off circle.

## Instructions

1. Shooter A passes the puck to shooter B outside the face-off circle. At the same time, the goaltender T-pushes out to the top of the crease and gets into a set position (G1 and G2).

2. Shooter B passes the puck to shooter C. The goaltender T-pushes across the crease, following the pass (G3).

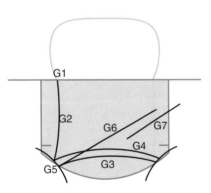

3. Shooter C passes the puck back to shooter B. The goaltender T-pushes back across the crease and follows the pass (G4).

4. Shooter B shoots the puck on the goaltender, and the goaltender makes a save on the shot (G5).

5. The goaltender executes an inside-edge push across to face shooter C (G6) while shooter C skates in and shoots the second puck on the goaltender. The goaltender makes a save on the shot (G7).

## Coaching Tips

- Beat the pass each time.
- Do not pull away from the save.
- Watch the puck in and out, but quickly lock your eyes on the second puck as you push across.

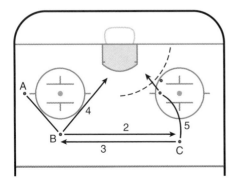

# Inside-Edge Push Into Far Post
# With Lead-Leg Recovery

## Purpose

This drill allows the goaltender to work on postsave recoveries to well-placed rebounds, followed by an inside-edge push to the post into a lean position and lead-leg recovery.

## Setup

The goaltender starts in a set position at the post (G1). Five shooters are needed. Shooter A is positioned at the half wall. Shooter B is positioned on the goal line beside the net. Shooter C is placed outside the face-off circle on the near side. Shooter D is positioned with a second puck on the goal line to the far side of the goaltender. Shooter E is outside the far face-off circle.

## Instructions

1. Shooter A passes the puck to shooter B.
2. Shooter B passes the puck to shooter C. The goaltender pushes out to the top of the crease (G2).

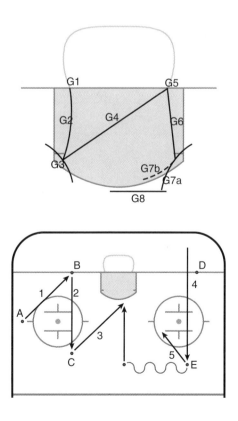

*(continued)*

# Inside-Edge Push Into Far Post
# With Lead-Leg Recovery *(continued)*

3. Shooter C takes a far-side shot on goal. The goaltender stops the shot (G3). The goaltender uses an inside-edge push to the far post in a butterfly (G4) and sets into a lean position on the post (G5).

4. Shooter D takes a second puck and passes to shooter E.

5. Shooter E has two options: He can either shoot from where the pass is received or he can skate into the middle and take a shot on goal. The goaltender uses a lead-leg recovery to push out to face shooter E (G6).

6. If the shot comes immediately off the pass, the goaltender makes the save (G7a), or he shuffles and follows the shooter into the middle to make the save (G7b), and then follows the rebound (G8).

## Coaching Tips

- Put the first shot into the corner with control each time the drill is performed.
- Never pull away from the puck.
- Push in a butterfly and reach with your lead toe toward the post while maintaining accuracy to effectively get to the far post.
- Maintain a strong seal on the post.
- Utilize active soft focus to the second shooter.

# Down and Up, Behind the Net
# With Breakaway

## Purpose

This drill allows the goaltender to focus on plays behind the net and defending in tight breakaways.

## Setup

The goaltender starts in a set position on the post. Four shooters are required. Shooter A is positioned at the half wall. Shooter B is on the goal line beside the net. Shooter C is at the top of the near face-off circle, and shooter D is at the top of the far-side face-off circle.

## Instructions

1. Shooter A passes the puck to shooter B. The goaltender starts at the post (G1).

2. Shooter B passes the puck to shooter C. At the same time as the pass is taking place, the goaltender T-pushes out to the top of the crease (G2).

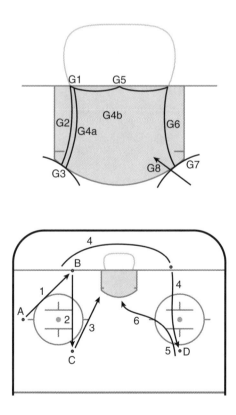

*(continued)*

# Down and Up, Behind the Net
# With Breakaway *(continued)*

3. Shooter C shoots short side on the goaltender, and the goaltender stops the shot (G3). If the goaltender gets back to the post on his feet, he will go from a wide position, creating a window over the short-side shoulder and into a lean (G4a). If the goaltender goes back to the post in a down position, he will go into a reach position (G4b) and then into a lean (G5).

4. Shooter B skates around the back of the net, picks up a second puck on the goal line, and passes the puck to shooter D. The goaltender performs a lead-leg recovery and pushes out to the top of the crease (G6). The goaltender does not come to a complete stop; he releases forward to face the breakaway (G7).

5. Shooter D skates in on a breakaway, and the goaltender then drifts back to follow the shooter on the breakaway (G8).

6. Shooter D shoots with intent to score.

## Coaching Tips

- If you stay down, make sure you get a tight seal on the post.
- Keep your eye on the puck as it is moved around the back of the net, using the 75-25 commitment tactic.
- Do not use hard C-cuts to defend the breakaway. Simply let momentum release you forward and backward as required.
- Use active soft focus throughout the drill.

# Post and Out Butterfly With Inside-Edge Push

## Purpose

This drill allows the goaltender to work on postsave recoveries by following and stopping in tight rebounds to either side.

## Setup

The goaltender starts at the post in a set position. One shooter is stationed in front of the crease with two pucks.

## Instructions

1. The goaltender T-pushes to the top of the crease.
2. The shooter shoots the puck directly into the goaltender's pads.
3. The goaltender drops into the butterfly to make the first save.
4. The shooter takes a second puck and pulls either right or left on the goaltender and then shoots. The goaltender inside-edge pushes to whichever side the shooter pulls the puck and makes the save.
5. The goaltender corrals and covers the loose puck.

## Coaching Tips

- Be patient. Push and stop, butterfly, and be aware of which direction the shooter is going to pull with the second shot.
- Watch the shooter's stick, determining to which side he will pull the second puck.
- Use path of direction when following the second shot.

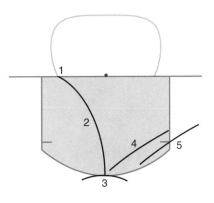

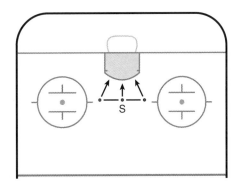

# Up, Across, and Back; Short-Side Shot; and Rebound

## Purpose

This drill presents game situations with passing and multiple shots. The goaltender will work on all the skills covered to this point in the book.

## Setup

The goaltender starts in a set position on the post (G1). Three shooters are needed. Shooter A is set up on the half wall with a puck, and a second puck is placed inside the face-off circle. Shooter B is placed in front of the near-side face-off circle. Shooter C is situated at the opposite far-side face-off circle.

## Instructions

1. Shooter A passes the puck to shooter B, and at the same time, the goaltender T-pushes to the top of the crease (G2).

2. Shooter B passes cross ice to shooter C. The goaltender T-pushes across the crease, following the pass (G3).

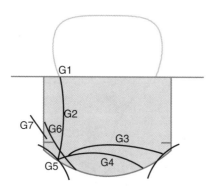

3. Shooter C passes back to shooter B. The goaltender T-pushes across the crease again, following the pass (G4).

4. Shooter B skates in past the face-off circle and shoots short side. The goaltender faces the shot from shooter B, ideally directing the rebound into the corner (G5).

5. The goaltender inside-edge pushes back toward the short-side post (G6).

6. Shooter A skates to the puck in the face-off circle and shoots with the intention to score. The goaltender faces the shot (G7).

## Coaching Tips

- Do not get overly aggressive in your pushes, or you will not be in an ideal position to face the second shot.
- Be sure to always beat the pass when following the cross-ice passes.

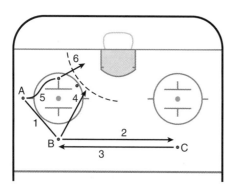

# Chapter 5
# Puck Handling

Chapter 4 focused on postsave recoveries, that is, the goaltender's ability to track a rebound and ready himself for the second shot. In that chapter, we discussed how to read the play and gauge whether to stay up or down after making the first save. We analyzed ideal methods of covering pucks and how to effectively utilize post leans for efficient movement across the crease. We concluded that, in its most simplistic form, the postsave recovery is the ability to follow a rebound. But what happens when the puck is shot into the defensive zone and there is no initial save to be made? What is the optimal way to get the puck out of the zone? This chapter discusses your role in handling the puck and assisting your teammates in clearing the defensive zone.

Puck handling has been a contentious issue for goaltenders for many years at both professional and amateur levels. Some coaches prefer their goaltenders to continuously come out and play the puck, acting as a third defenseman. Other coaches want their goalies to be more conservative by simply stopping and leaving the puck for their defensemen. The latter tend to believe that skaters are better equipped to make zone-clearing plays, as opposed to the goaltender, who is weighed down by cumbersome equipment.

We have seen a recent trend in which goaltenders are becoming more efficient at handling and moving the puck with speed and accuracy. In the past, puck handling used to be a small part of goaltending camps, but it is now a main focus. In fact, this past year, Eli Wilson Goaltending added puck handling–only camps to its repertoire. Currently, goaltenders at all levels are quickly becoming more adept at handling the puck, providing outlet passes to their defensemen and forwards and in many cases controlling the flow of the game.

In this chapter, we focus on the key elements that make up an effective puck-handling goaltender. We concentrate on different types of situations you may face and how to play the puck most effectively with accuracy and efficiency. The chapter concludes with a progressive series of drills that will allow you to work on all the skills discussed.

# CHARACTERISTICS OF AN EFFECTIVE PUCK-HANDLING GOALTENDER

There are five main components that make an effective puck-handling goaltender. As a goaltender, you must be able to do the following:

### Think and move your feet at the same time.

In many instances, you will come out to play the puck. You will scan the ice and decide on your best option. Being able to combine hard focus, soft focus, and decision making, all while moving your feet, can be a challenge. An inefficient puck-handling goaltender freezes his feet when making a play to move the puck up ice. As the goaltender approaches the puck, he starts to think about what he is going to do with it. While thinking, he stops moving his feet, and opposition forecheckers can then disrupt the play. It is important to look up ice and keep your feet moving in the same direction. This allows you to see the entire ice and make the best play with the puck. Repeating skating pattern drills allow you to react to a play without thinking about it. Skating patterns are discussed later in this chapter.

### Point and move your feet up ice.

It is essential that you always have your feet pointed up ice. This allows you a full view of the ice surface and the ability to look for the best play option and potential threats. You should always attempt to make plays up ice. Playing the puck backward can lead to disastrous and sometimes embarrassing results.

### Transition efficiently to two hands on the stick.

For most puck playing, you need to be adept at getting both hands on your stick prior to making a play. Having both hands on the stick provides both power and control. You can utilize the overhand or underhand grip to make a pass or shoot the puck out of the defensive zone. Overhand and underhand grips are described later in this chapter. In either case, the transition from one hand to two hands on the stick should be seamless.

### Move the puck to the forehand whenever possible.

Although there are times when you will be forced to make a backhand play, most of the time it is best to transition the puck from the backhand to the forehand. The puck is easier to control on the forehand, and often, passes are more accurate because you can see the play in front of you. Backhand passes can be made, but remember you may be blind to the developments on one-half of the ice. For this reason, we emphasize that you should try to make plays on the forehand whenever possible. When you make a forehand pass, you're facing the play; on a backhand pass, your back is to the play, and you can see only the ice in the direction you're making the pass to. You are blind to the one side of the ice when you are making passes off the backhand, and that's why it is better to play off the forehand.

### Communicate with teammates.

Skaters give goalies instructions on what to do with the puck while goalies alert the skaters to potential threats behind them. It is important for you to get comfortable with your teammates and learn their tendencies and preferences. You should learn which players want to come behind the net to pick up the puck and which ones want to receive passes in the corners or up the ice. It is important to know whether your players want passes on their forehands or backhands. Verbal communication and eye contact between you and the players are key. Language used between defensemen and goalies should be as simple as possible, for example, leave it, over, or rim.

## The Martin Brodeur Rule

Martin Brodeur has been thought by many to be the finest puck-handling goaltender of all time, so much so that when the NHL decided at the start of the 2005–2006 season to introduce the trapezoid rule, many among hockey's elite referred to it as the Brodeur rule. The trapezoid is the area between the two markings illustrated in figure 5.1. The goaltender is limited to playing the puck within the trapezoid area or in front of the goal line only. If the goaltender plays the puck outside of the trapezoid and below the goal line, he is automatically assessed a two-minute delay of game penalty.

The rule was brought into the game to open up the ice and increase scoring by limiting how much a goalie could play the puck. Since that time, goaltenders have adapted to the rule and are continuously working on ways to become more proficient at handling the puck.

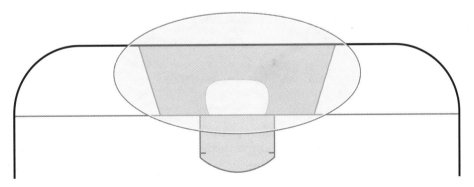

**Figure 5.1**   The area between the two lines is the trapezoid, where the goaltender is allowed to play the puck.

# EFFECTIVE PUCK-HANDLING SKILLS

With the speed of the game today, a goaltender who can effectively play the puck is a huge asset to his team. An effective puck-handling goaltender can help his team by moving the puck out of the defensive zone quickly. A goaltender can make simple plays with the puck that allow his defensemen more time to break out of the zone. An effective puck-handling goaltender acts as a third defenseman. A good transition game will generate more offensive opportunities at the other end of the ice.

At the highest levels of hockey, there are set plays where your ability to move the puck quickly and accurately plays an essential role.

## Gripping the Stick

There are two types of grips you can use when playing the puck: the overhand and the underhand grip. Very few goaltenders use the underhand grip in the game today. The overhand grip requires less strength, and the stick can be used as leverage to get power behind your pass. The overhand grip allows you the advantage of using the flexibility of your stick to make crisper, harder passes. The underhand grip can be better when putting the puck up ice because you can get underneath the puck and get height on your shot.

### Overhand Grip

The difference between the two grips is in the placement of the lower, or glove, hand. In the overhand grip, the glove hand is placed over the top of the shaft of the stick (figure 5.2). It is important that you use a firm grip, applying pressure on the thumb of your catching hand. The advantages of the overhand grip follow:

- Allows you to use the stick and glove as leverage by pushing down on the ice and forward on the puck. This grip does not require as much physical strength as does the underhand grip.
- Excellent for short passes. You can apply a quick, snapping motion to pass the puck.
- Puts you in a very natural shooting position.

### Underhand Grip

The underhand grip is used to shoot the puck (figure 5.3). Compared to the overhand grip, moving the puck with the underhand grip requires more physical strength and skill. In the underhand grip, reach around the bottom of your stick and firmly place your glove on the underside of the stick and squeeze. Then, put pressure down on the ice and snap your hands forward to get the puck off your stick. Because of its cumbersome nature, as the game

Figure 5.2    The overhand grip.

Figure 5.3    The underhand grip.

of hockey continues to progress, the underhand grip is being used less regularly. The advantages of the underhand grip follow:

- It is better for shooting the puck and executing long passes.
- It may be used for shooting the puck out of the defensive zone.

# Passing the Puck

When you are adept at passing, your team has a distinct advantage. Goalies who can pass the puck are able to clear the zone and often provide scoring opportunities for teammates transitioning into the offensive zone. There are three basic steps to accurate passing:

1. Ensure you have a strong bottom hand on the stick. For passing, the overhand grip is recommended.

2. Point your feet at your intended target to ensure an accurate pass.

3. With your lower hand over the top of the stick, scan the ice to see available options and choose the easiest option, focusing on short passes. Then, snap the pass to your teammate.

# Playing Rims

Generally, anytime there is a shot around the boards from outside the blue line, you should leave the net to play the puck. Playing the puck can be anything as simple as stopping it and leaving it for a teammate to executing a long pass up ice and creating an offensive opportunity. In most instances, you are required to control the puck and make effective plays to clear the defensive zone. Although stopping rims and effectively playing the puck can be challenging, it is a skill that must be continually practiced and improved.

Remember, the decision on whether to play the puck or leave it depends on how quickly the play is developing and what your teammate is communicating to you. If the play develops slowly, you have more time to scan the ice and consider your options. On a fast-developing play, you will need to rely more heavily on communication with teammates. We cannot overstate the importance of being aware of your teammates' tendencies and how effective communication can result in a successful play up ice.

## Stopping a Rim

In the past, many coaches thought the most effective way to stop a rim was for the goaltender to get his entire body against the boards and funnel the puck between his skate and the wall (figure 5.4). This is not a good practice to follow because this technique can result in the puck's bouncing off your skate and out of control. There are instances, however, where a rim comes in extremely hard and you will need your full body for reinforcement. Although not recommended on a regular basis, stopping the puck using the body is a skill that can be worked on in moderation.

Goaltenders are becoming more adept at handling rims using just their sticks. This is the preferred method of handling a rim as opposed to the whole-body technique (figure 5.5). By using just the stick, you gain control and can always track the puck. From there, you can easily make a play up

Figure 5.4    Stopping a rim with the body.

Figure 5.5    Stopping a rim with the stick.

ice or leave the puck for a teammate. When building puck-handling skills, it is essential that you practice stopping rims using just your stick.

After successfully stopping a rim, you have numerous options with the puck.

**Stop It Dead**    When a hard rim comes around, get behind the middle of the net, stop the puck completely, and leave it for your defenseman. Ideally, you should get directly behind the net to leave the option open to play the puck to either side. However, on a hard rim, sometimes it is more efficient for you to meet the puck on the strong side, providing the opportunity to make a play more quickly.

**Touch and Move**    When the rim comes in on your backhand, the touch-and-move technique requires you to stop the puck dead, pull it off the wall, and send it to your defenseman in one continuous motion. The key to this tactic is to stop and move the puck quickly without breaking skating stride.

**Keep the Rim Going**    In some instances, you may choose to keep the rim going at an accelerated pace. Instead of stopping the rim, simply continue the puck around the boards or make a direct pass to a teammate. You must carry this tactic out in one fluid motion.

**Set the Puck**    When the rim comes around the boards, you can set the puck for a teammate. You stop the puck and pull it off the wall, making it accessible to your teammate's forehand. Then, you must quickly get back into the net. You can enter the net on either side, whichever is faster. The quicker way can be determined either by amount of ice you have to cover or by which side your momentum takes you to.

## Rims to the Forehand Side

When a rim comes around to your forehand (figure 5.6), you must make some quick decisions. Where is the optimal position to make first contact with the puck? Do I stop the puck and play it up ice or simply leave it for my defenseman? Whether you play the puck up ice or leave it for your defenseman is dependent on the pressure the opposition is providing with the forecheck. If there is very little pressure from the opposition, you can stop the puck for your defenseman and let him orchestrate the play out of the defensive zone. When more pressure is applied, you can either move the puck up ice to a defenseman, provided he is open, or get the puck out of your own zone to alleviate the pressure.

If you stop the puck directly behind the middle of the net, you then have the option to play the puck to either side or simply leave it for your defenseman and then get back into the net. Strategic positioning deters opposition players from pressuring the goalie behind the net. A barrier is created by the net, allowing you more time to set up plays or draw an opposition fore-

Figure 5.6   The goaltender stops the puck on his forehand.

checker out of position. In this situation, as the rim approaches, position yourself directly behind the net and place your stick firmly against the wall to meet the oncoming puck (figure 5.7). Once the puck has been controlled, you can either pivot and play the puck up ice, or stop it, leave it for your defenseman, and get back into your net.

Although stopping the puck directly behind the net is the preferred method, there are occasions with a hard rim where you will meet the puck on the strong side prior to its going directly behind the net. The strong side is the side the puck is coming from. For example, if a shot comes around the boards on your glove-hand side, that is the strong side. The weak side would be the opposite side, so you may play the puck to that side to alleviate pressure. Although meeting the puck early can be an efficient method to make a quick pass to a teammate, it also limits your options. That's why we encourage you to set up behind the center of the net.

## Rims to the Backhand Side

Backhand rims are handled quite differently than those that come to the forehand. Some of the principles that apply to backhand rims also apply to their forehand counterparts. When stopping a puck on the backhand, you

**Figure 5.7**  The goaltender stops the puck directly behind the net.

should try to use your momentum to pivot and transition the puck to the forehand whenever possible. However, if you have no other choice, as the rim approaches, position yourself directly behind the net and using the top hand to guide, jam the toe of your stick firmly against the boards to create a blockade (refer to figure 5.5; this is also the backhand). Once in possession of the puck, position your body so you have the option to play the puck to either side.

## Head Fakes and Look-Offs

Just as players use moves to throw the opposition out of position, you can do the same thing by creating more time and space for yourself. When the opposition forechecker approaches, you can create time and space by faking to move in one direction and then going the opposite direction. This is known as a look-off. Similarly, a head fake is a simple movement of the head one way making the opponent think you are going in that direction with the puck and then playing it in the opposite direction. Other fakes include but are not limited to the following:

- Pretending to pass one way and then sending the pass the other way
- Dropping a shoulder to fake a shot
- Fanning the stick past the puck

# Playing Dump-Ins

Opposition teams often dump the puck into the defensive zone either to change lines or to forecheck and create a turnover. Dump-ins can be either on goal or wide of the goal. There are different techniques that you must apply for each type of dump-in.

## Dump-Ins on Goal

No goaltender wants the starring role on the bloopers highlight reel. Yet nothing can fool a goaltender like a long dump-in on goal. If the puck bounces and isn't played correctly, it can end up in the back of the net. Dump-ins can come from far out and approach you along the ice or high in the air. You need to play each variation of the dump-in a little differently.

- When a long dump-in shot approaches the net, you must come out at the puck and butterfly so it doesn't skip over you and into the goal.
- When a dump-in comes along the ice, you want to back up your stick with your glove. Once you have control of the puck, you can make a play up ice.
- When a dump-in on goal is high, you should catch the puck and bring your glove to the ice with momentum so the puck lays flat. Never drop the puck from waist height, as it may bounce unpredictably when it lands.

## Dump-Ins to the Stick Side

Dump-ins to the stick side can create confusion for goaltenders. You must decide how you want to play the dump-in; your approach will change depending on the puck's proximity to the net. Because of the trapezoid rule, any puck traveling into the corner must be stopped above the red line or else you cannot play it. These variables can create hesitation you on how to best play the puck.

There are gray areas on how you play the dump-in because it depends on the pressure the opposition forwards are applying. Lots of pressure means you have less time to play the puck and may simply cover it for a whistle. Other gray areas are dependent on the speed at which the puck is traveling on the dump-in. If the puck comes in quickly, you will have more time with it because it comes to you faster than the opposing, forechecking players. Endless scenarios are possible, so we included only the most common. We divided the ice surface into three zones: the reinforcement zone, the forehand zone, and the paddle-down zone (figure 5.8). As a guideline, each zone has different tactics on how to best play the puck.

**Reinforcement Zone**    The reinforcement zone is the area either directly on goal or close to it (figure 5.8). When a dump-in comes anywhere in the reinforcement zone, you must cautiously handle the puck by backing up your

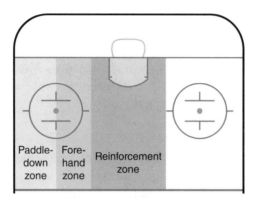

Figure 5.8    Stick-side zones.

stick with the glove (figure 5.9*a*), body, or a combination of both. In some cases, the paddle-down technique may be required. All pucks that are in the reinforcement zone need to be handled with a hard focus on the puck. After the puck has been stopped and controlled, you can then scan the ice to make the optimal play. Once the puck has been stopped dead, if the best play is to your forehand, make sure to step back from the puck and move it directly on your forehand (figure 5.9*b*).

There are instances where your optimal play is to make a quick forward outlet pass with one hand on the stick (figure 5.10), for example, when the defenseman is skating quickly back toward you and you can get the puck up to him quickly. You do not have to take the time to stop the puck, transition to two hands on the stick, and play it forward. Simply stop it and play it up to the defenseman. In other cases, your best option may be to make an indirect pass off the backboards to the far side and onto the stick of a teammate. For example, if the opposition forecheck is applying pressure on the strong side, you can simply play it off the backboards to a teammate on the weak side.

**Forehand Zone**    The forehand zone is the midway portion between the goal and the corner of the ice. Dump-ins to this zone are within range for you to beat the puck to the goal line without having to extend your body while still ending up with the puck on your forehand. For dump-ins in this zone, leave your net quickly to intercept the puck before it crosses the goal line, skate past the puck as it approaches, and turn your body to receive the puck on your forehand (figure 5.11). Then, check available play options, communicate with your teammates, and move the puck.

Figure 5.9   The goaltender *(a)* reinforces the stick with his glove and *(b)* transitions to make a play from his forehand.

Figure 5.10   A goaltender makes a quick outlet pass.

Figure 5.11    The goaltender skates past the puck to play it from the forehand.

**Paddle-Down Zone**    The paddle-down zone is the area beside the net near the far corner of the ice. To play the puck, you must meet it before it crosses the red line; otherwise, you are outside the trapezoid area and will end up with a penalty if you play the puck. Stopping the puck above the red line is accomplished by utilizing the paddle-down-above-the-goal-line technique. To execute this, from a semi-down position, stop the puck above the goal line using an extended reverse paddle-down position (figure 5.12*a*), and then get up and rotate over the front of the puck, bringing the puck to the forehand (figure 5.12*b*). Once the puck is in control on the forehand, you have several options. In one fluid motion, you can move the puck up ice to a teammate (figure 5.12*c*) or simply make a quick, short outlet pass. The third option is to stop the puck and set it up for a teammate.

When stopping and playing the puck from the paddle zone, the following tactics apply:

- Get an early read on your play options.
- Make sure your paddle is flat on the ice.
- Make sure your timing is such that you stop the puck with the paddle of your stick.

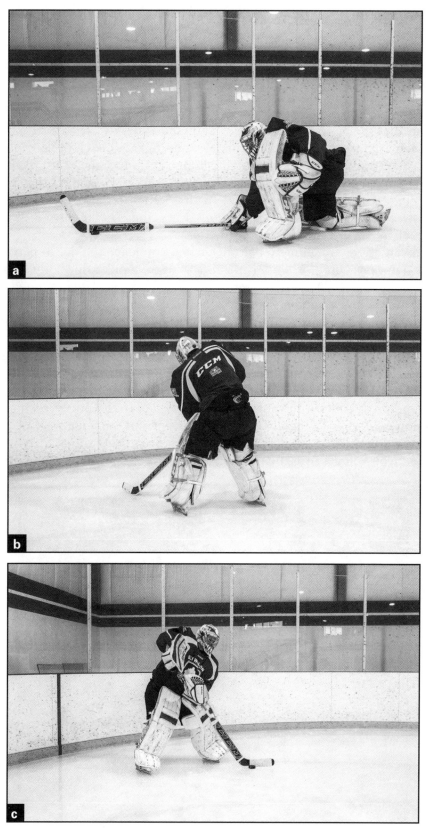

Figure 5.12 A goaltender *(a)* stops the puck above the red line, applying the paddle-down technique; *(b)* rotates his body in front of the puck to his forehand; and *(c)* makes a clean play up ice.

# LEAVING AND RETURNING TO THE NET

If you do not get out of your net to play the rim quickly enough, you will miss the rim, and the opposition could get to the puck first. Getting back into the net efficiently is key. If you play the puck but don't get back in your net and there is a turnover, the opponent can simply shoot the puck into the empty net. When leaving the net to bear down on a rim, it is essential that you always skate quickly and with purpose (figure 5.13). You must be able to read the puck's trajectory to anticipate where it is going. The key is not to freeze your feet as you are thinking about the play.

Be aware there are going to be times when you leave the net to play a rim and you miss it. Often, when a rim gets past a goaltender, his body language will change because of the dejection of missing the puck. The key when missing the rim is to stay composed and focused and quickly get back into your net. The last thing you want is to hesitate when entering the goal, giving the opposition a clear shot on the empty net.

Similarly, there is a recommended technique for returning to the net. In the past, it was believed that a goalie should go back into the net on the same side he exited. However, this is no longer the case. It is more efficient for you to enter the net on the side of the goal you play the puck or whichever direction continues the momentum of your current movement. It is important for you to have a sense of urgency when reentering the net. By cutting the post, you will get into the net efficiently without getting tangled up with

Figure 5.13  A goaltender exits the net to play the rim.

other players or mixed up in the play. Another tactic goaltenders use when reentering the net is to set a pick. When setting a pick, your aim is to slightly interfere with the opposing forechecker and gain extra time for your teammates to move the puck up ice.

## Cutting the Post

Cutting the post is the concept of getting in and out of your net using the most efficient skating pattern possible. When entering or exiting, rather than taking a wide turn by the net, it is best to skate as close to the post as possible (figure 5.14), called "cutting the post," and then get back into the net in a ready position in case there is a turnover. This enables you to enter and exit the net with the utmost efficiency.

## Setting a Pick

A pick is a form of interference that, if done subtly, can be used as an effective tool to slow opposition forwards on the forecheck. As you exit the net to stop the rim for your defenseman and after setting the puck, simply take a little more time getting back to your net. Then, given the opportunity, bump into, or "pick," the opposing forechecker. The pick relieves the pressure of the forecheck, allowing the defenseman more time to make a play with the puck.

Figure 5.14   A goaltender reenters the net, skating as close to the post as possible.

When setting a pick, don't cut the post. Instead, come in a little wider and apply a simple bump of the opposing forechecker to slow him up and cut off his direct path to your defenseman. By pure definition of the rules, it is interference, but this is a very subtle form of interference that will not be called by the referee.

# PUCK-HANDLING DRILLS

Since there are so many variables involved with handling the puck, you must continually hone your skills. You should work on repetitive skating patterns that simulate puck play situations during every practice. When performing puck-handing drills, it is important that you pay attention to all the minute details. Are you skating to the puck with speed, confidence, and power? Are you working on stopping the puck with your stick only, or do you find yourself reinforcing rims by using your body? Do you scan the ice to see available play options? Do you communicate with your teammates? Do you take time to study your teammate's tendencies?

The following progressive drills allow you to work on all the skills and techniques discussed in this chapter. Starting with simple passing drills and skating patterns, we progress to intricate zone-clearing and dump-in drills. Remember to pay attention to detail, always performing each drill with speed, accuracy, and purpose.

# Forehand and Backhand Pass Drill

## Purpose

This drill provides two goaltenders the opportunity to simultaneously work on making and taking passes on the forehand and backhand. The goaltenders work on their speed when transitioning from forehand to backhand and vice versa.

## Setup

Two goaltenders are required for this drill. Goaltenders are set up facing each other at the same cross-ice distance as the face-off dots.

## Instructions

1. Goaltender A makes a forehand pass to goaltender B.
2. Goaltender B receives the pass on the forehand and makes a forehand pass back to goaltender A.
3. The drill continues with the goaltenders alternating between forehand and backhand passes. Goaltenders can receive passes on their backhand and transition to the forehand and vice versa.
4. Improvisations can be made to this drill whereby goaltender A passes the puck high to goaltender B. Goaltender B catches the puck, sets it down, and makes a high pass to goaltender A.
5. The distance between the goaltenders can be lengthened or shortened. A shorter distance between the two means the goaltenders must make quick transitions between receiving the puck and passing it. A longer distance between the two means the goaltenders will have to make long, accurate passes.

## Coaching Tips

- After you make the pass, return to regular stick position. This entails moving from two hands back to one hand on the stick. Ensure that you make this transition after every pass.
- Make sure all passes are hard, crisp, and accurate.
- When the goalies stand far apart, they are working on their passing skills. When they stand closer together, they are working on their receiving skills.

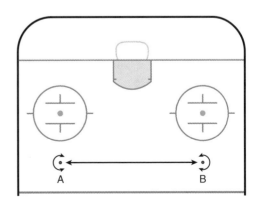

# Three-Way Pass Drill

## Purpose

This drill allows goaltenders to work on hand and foot speed, pivoting, making and receiving high and low passes, eye-hand coordination, and touch and move. All puck-handling skills can be incorporated into this drill by doing different variations of it. Creativity is a key factor in this drill.

## Setup

Three goaltenders are required for this drill. The three goaltenders line up cross ice with goaltender B positioning himself in the middle of goaltenders A and C.

## Instructions

1. Goaltender A passes to goaltender B, who transitions either to forehand or backhand and passes to goaltender C.
2. A variation is goaltender B lies down in the middle of goaltenders A and B. Goaltender A sends a saucer pass to goaltender C. Goaltender C then saucer passes to goaltender A.

## Coaching Tips

- Be creative. Work on forehand, backhand, and saucer passes.
- Ensure the goaltender in the middle turns and pivots before passing.
- All goaltenders must return to regular stick position after *each* pass they make.

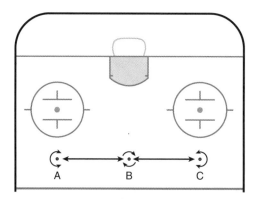

# Skating Patterns

## Purpose

This drill allows goaltenders to work on all the skating patterns involved in playing the puck. The drill consists of mirror plays without a puck, starting with basic movements from the net to the boards and back into the net and progressing to turns and pivots. Goaltenders work on repetitive skating movements so they become a natural response for the goaltender when faced with puck-handling situations in a game.

## Setup

The goaltender sets in a ready position at the post.

## Instruction

1. The goaltender goes behind the net and simulates stopping and playing the puck and then enters the net on the opposite side.
2. The goaltender continues to simulate different plays, stopping the puck on the forehand and backhand and passing in both directions.

## Coaching Tips

- Simulate game situations.
- Simulate a different play each time, for example, touch and go, and pivot and pass on forehand and backhand.
- Be sure the goaltender cuts the post and enters the net on the correct side each time.

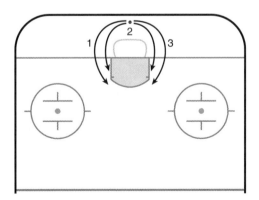

# Dump-In Drill

## Purpose

This drill provides the goaltender the opportunity to work on stopping pucks dumped in directly on net and passing the puck out to moving targets. The puck may be shot in along the ice or dumped in high to the goaltender.

## Setup

The goaltender starts in the middle of his net at the top of the crease facing the puck carrier. This drill requires two shooters. Shooter A has a puck and is stationed in the center of the ice just outside the blue line. Shooter B is positioned at the blue line without a puck.

## Instructions

1. Shooter A dumps the puck in at the goalie. The dump-in can be either along the ice or in the air.

2. The goaltender handles the dump-in. If it is a high dump, he catches the puck and sets it on the ice. If the dump is along the ice, he stops it with the stick and rotates into position to make a pass to shooter B.

3. Shooter B skates from the blue line around and through the face-off circle. At the same time, the goaltender gains control of the puck and passes it to shooter B as he crosses through the face-off circle. Shooter B accepts the pass from the goaltender and proceeds to pass the puck up ice to shooter A.

## Coaching Tips

- If the puck is dumped in high and caught, make sure the puck is set on the ice with momentum so it doesn't bounce.

- Make sure passes are crisp. Do not pass the puck into the players' feet.

- Make sure to control the first shot cleanly to move it up ice as quickly as possible. Do not be casual with the puck.

- Make sure to communicate with the players on the ice.

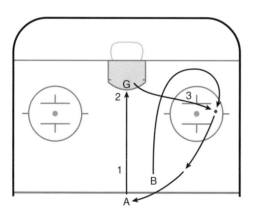

# Clearing the Zone

## Purpose

This drill works on the goaltender's ability to make a read on the play and stop the puck above the goal line by utilizing the backhand paddle-down technique. This drill requires the goaltender to practice long passes. The concept of this drill is for the goaltender to work on being able to get the puck out of the defensive zone on to the stick of a teammate and catch the opposition off guard during a line change.

## Setup

The goaltender starts in the middle of the crease facing the puck carrier. Two shooters are required. Shooter A is stationed in the middle of the ice outside of the blue line. Shooter B is set outside of the blue line along the wall.

## Instructions

1. Shooter A shoots the puck toward the corner of the ice.
2. The goaltender skates out and stops the puck in the corner without letting it pass the red line.
3. The goaltender turns, pivots, and passes the puck out to shooter B and then returns to the net.
4. Shooter B accepts the pass from the goaltender between the blue line and center ice.

## Coaching Tips

- Be fluid in movement.
- Try to stop the puck and play it up ice in a continuous motion.
- Quick feet are essential to stop the puck before it crosses the red line.

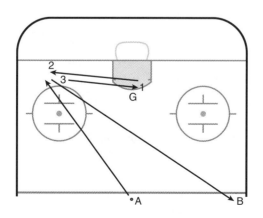

# Rims With Options

## Purpose

This drill provides the goaltender the opportunity to work on stopping rims, setting up pucks, and making passes.

## Setup

The goaltender starts in a set position at the top of the crease facing shooter A, who is positioned just outside of the blue line at the left point. Shooters B and C are positioned just outside their respective face-off circles near the boards.

## Instructions

1. Shooter A rims the puck in from just outside the blue line.
2. The goaltender moves behind the net to stop the puck.
3. Shooters B and C wait for the goaltender to stop the rim behind the net and pass the puck to either shooter.
4. Shooters B and C should be communicating with the goaltender as soon as he moves out to stop the rim.
5. The goaltender sets the puck and passes to either shooter B or C. The goaltender has the option to make the pass from either the forehand or backhand.
6. The shooter who received the puck from the goaltender passes it back to shooter A to start the drill again.

## Coaching Tips

- Treat the drill like a game situation and perform all movements with purpose.
- Get your stick ready to stop the puck.
- Communicate with the shooters who are awaiting the pass.
- Always scan the ice while skating.
- Repeat the drill from the opposite side of the ice.
- Shooters B and C can be replaced by goaltenders to provide more opportunity for goaltenders to receive and make passes.

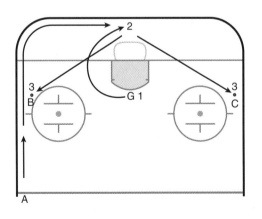

# Chapter 6
# Tactics

The previous chapters focused on how to prepare for and execute a save. We discussed what to do after making the first save and how to best prepare for a second and third shot. We analyzed the optimal ways to corral and cover loose pucks or direct pucks out of play to force stoppages. In chapter 5, we concentrated on puck handling. We talked about the goaltender's role in handling the puck and clearing the defensive zone. We discussed the components that make an effective puck-handling goaltender and analyzed the types of rims and how to best handle them. We focused on how to properly execute short and long pass plays between the goaltender and his teammates. We concluded that communication between the goaltender and his defensemen is a necessary component to becoming a successful puck-handling goaltender.

The last four chapters discussed the tools necessary to perform the basic functions required of a goaltender. However, as we stated earlier, there are no absolutes in hockey. Defensive miscues, deflected shots, "funny" bounces off the boards, penalty calls, odd-man rush situations, and scramble plays often lead to unpredictable results.

A goaltender playing against any offensive attack must incorporate mental, physical, and tactical skills. Are you in the moment? Are you conscious of your body positioning and aware of where the opposing shooters are? Are you focused on the puck? From there, you begin to make reads and see how the play may transpire. Many goaltenders will focus on one component but not the other. They may concentrate on the puck but not on themselves or vice versa. Many things need to tie together in a goaltender's mind so he can effectively react to situations. Goaltenders need to have a systematic approach and a consistent mindset so they can react instinctively as plays develop.

This chapter is about playing the game and defending the unforeseen. Here, we determine what skills to use at what time to defend various situations. This chapter focuses on odd-man rushes, including breakaways; penalty shots; and two-on-one, two-on-none, and three-on-two situations. We also delve into power play defense and support, tips and deflections, screens, and scramble plays. We also briefly touch on the goaltender's thought process in any given state (goaltender's mindset will be discussed in greater detail in chapter 8).

# BREAKAWAYS

A breakaway occurs when a shooter comes in one-on-one with the goaltender. It is one of the most exciting plays in the game. Breakaways can be generated off either wing or straight up the center of the ice. NHL goaltenders can go for several games without facing a clear-cut breakaway.

## Gap Control

From a goaltender's perspective, gap control is about matching the shooter's speed and controlling the space between himself and the shooter. This is particularly important when facing a breakaway. If the shooter gets too close to you, he can make a move in tight and get around you. As you back into your net, if there is too much space between you and the shooter, the shooter will be able to see larger portions of exposed net in which to shoot the puck. When considering gap control, you want to maximize your coverage by controlling the space of the gap between you and the shooter. Here are a few things to keep in mind:

- Be in good position in terms of the space between you and the shooter, and hold that position.
- Wait out the shooter.
- The best shooting position on the ice is the slot. The best defense for a goaltender against a shot from the slot is to be at the top of the blue paint. Use that gauge as a starting point for gap control and match the opposition's speed from there.
- Be patient and control your timing.

The thought still exists that when facing an odd-man rush, the goaltender should perform a hard C-cut to move out and a hard C-cut backward to maintain gap control with the shooter. Instead, it is more effective if you transfer your weight to push out and release forward. By releasing forward, we mean you let your momentum carry you forward—more like drifting forward rather than digging in to the ice with your blade to perform a hard C-cut. The same goes for the backward movement. Simply transfer your weight, release your feet backward, and allow yourself to drift. This movement is much more efficient than the C-cut. At the NHL level, goaltenders no longer hard C-cut out or back to control the gap. Previously, when goaltenders would perform the hard C-cut to move backward, they would be off balance and not squared up to the shooter properly. Now, with the weight transfer, you simply back up, remaining balanced and squared up to the shooter.

# Types of Breakaways

We consider two types of breakaways: from the middle of the ice or from either wing. When you identify a pending breakaway, it is important to position yourself at the top of the crease and ready yourself for either a shot or a deke by the opposing player. We also briefly discuss a short breakaway, such as on a defensive turnover, where the breakaway starts from in tight and the goaltender has less time to prepare.

## Straight-On Breakaway

An opponent who has a straight-on breakaway is not approaching the goal on an angle; he is centered between the goalposts. He approaches the goaltender straight up the ice through the slot. When the shooter gets to the slot, the goaltender needs to be at the top of the paint. A forward trying to score on a breakaway will attempt to throw off the goaltender's gap control and timing, so you need to get out and in position to control the gap (figure 6.1). You need to keep your stick lined up on the puck and face the blade of your stick at the puck. The stick then acts as a guide to keep you under control and your body centered on the puck. Wherever the puck goes, your stick goes.

It is also important for you to get a read on the opposing shooter. Is he going to shoot or is he deking? If the puck is in front of the shooter, he is in a position where he can't shoot, so prepare to play the deke (more about this

**Figure 6.1** The goaltender positions himself at the top of the crease to face the straight-on breakaway.

later). If the puck is beside the shooter, he is in a position to shoot but can still bring the puck in front of himself to deke you. If the player chooses to shoot, it is essential that you close the five-hole as quickly as possible. The five-hole is the open space between your pads. You close it by dropping into a butterfly with the knees tight together and maintaining your stick in proper position in front of you.

If the player dekes, use your edges and move into a butterfly slide to follow the shooter to either side. Make sure to have enough backward momentum to enable yourself to slide to either post to make the save. If the butterfly is not covering enough of the net, you will need to extend your body to make the save.

### Goaltender Tips: Straight-On Breakaway

- Be at the top of your crease and move out slightly to face the shooter.
- Keep your stick on the ice.
- Dig your skate in and transfer your weight to gain backward momentum so you can start controlling the gap between you and the shooter.
- When the shooter gets into the slot, your heels should be at the top of the paint.
- Read the shooter to determine whether he is going to shoot or deke.

## Breakaway From the Wing

When a breakaway develops with the shooter coming down the wing, the goaltender applies the same principles that apply to the straight-on break-away, except the shooter will be more prone to deke the goaltender. It is important for you to be aware of whether the shooter shoots right or left handed. Read the play to determine whether the shooter will deke to his forehand or backhand. A shooter coming in on an angle has less net to shoot at than if he were approaching straight on. For this reason, he will choose to use a deke to try to move you laterally and make you more vulnerable by opening you up. You need to be aware of which way the opposing forward is going to deke so you can move with the play to stop the puck. You need to have awareness and be prepared to defend the play you face.

On a breakaway from the side, you will need to have more backward momentum and speed so you can get fully across your crease to the opposite post should the shooter choose that path. Regardless of whether the breakaway is from the blocker or glove side, you will use the same tactics to defend it.

### Goaltender Tips: Breakaway From the Wing

- Maintain gap control. It is the number one key to making the save.
- Follow the puck with your stick. This enables you to keep your body over the puck, keeping you in the center of the net.

## Short Breakaways

If the puck is turned over allowing the opposition a breakaway in tight, you will need to react quickly. If possible, move out, hold your position, and make a quick read on whether the shooter is going to shoot or deke. Apply the same tactics as you would if it were a breakaway from farther out.

# DEKES

A deke occurs when an opposing player stickhandles the puck to open up a goaltender and make him vulnerable by getting him moving in the wrong direction. The attacker attempts to make a scoring chance available that wouldn't normally be there from a straight-on shot. When defending an opposition deke, you must step out to the top of the crease and when the player begins to deke, use your edges in control and butterfly slides to follow to either side and extend into a save position. Keep your head over the puck and your shoulders forward to cover the vertical angles. By vertical angles, we mean that you are playing over the top of the puck with the upper body to take away space from the top half of the net. You should not lean back when sliding across; you always want to be playing with your head and upper body over the top of the puck. You then release back with enough momentum to move to either post with the shooter; simply transfer your weight, release your feet backward, and allow yourself to drift (figure 6.2).

## Poke Check

There are situations when you can catch a player with his head down, providing an opportunity to knock the puck off his stick. The poke check can be a dangerous tactic to use because if you fully extend your arm and miss the puck, you leave yourself at the mercy of the shooter. If the shooter pulls around the poke check, you are completely committed and exposed, and the opponent will easily score. Instead, use the nonextending poke check; move your forearm forward and jab at the puck with a quick motion without extending your hand up the shaft of the stick.

## Defending Penalty Shots

On a penalty shot, you can't leave the crease until the opposing player crosses the blue line, so you will have to make a judgment on his speed and adapt accordingly. If the shooter comes down the wing, you need to maintain good gap control, be conscious of angles, and not get pulled out of position. You need to maintain good balance and be patient to try to determine what the shooter is going to do. Some shooters will come in on a penalty shot extremely slowly to throw off your gap control. You, too, must move slowly and be prepared to pick up speed should the shooter do so. You don't want to back up so quickly that you end up in the net.

Figure 6.2 The goaltender *(a)* starts backward momentum and *(b)* prepares to play the deke.

Although the penalty shot appears to be exactly like a breakaway, it is different because there is no backcheck applied to the shooter, so he has a lot of time to analyze the situation and make a move on you. Since the implementation of shootouts to decide tie games, the penalty shot is not as rare an occurrence as it once was. Shooters at the NHL level are constantly working on their moves to improve their odds of scoring in shootouts. Since there is no backcheck on a penalty shot, the shooter has far more control over what he can do with the puck. The key for you is to remain calm and wait out the shooter.

The perception is that a shooter who scores by deking on breakaways has great hands when really it is about the shooter's edge control and the rate at which he changes speeds to throw off your gap control. Goaltenders who are successful at stopping penalty shots are the ones who can adapt quickly to the shooter's change of direction and speed. If the shooter decides to shoot, be at the top of the paint when the opponent arrives into the slot. Hold your position, and be ready to react. Be prepared to quickly close your five-hole to make the save.

# POWER PLAY

It has been said many times that the goaltender must be the team's best penalty killer. This is true in many respects. Most teams have a first and second power play unit, and usually, the power play units have different tactics for scoring. It is important for you to understand each team's first and second power play units. Your awareness of what the opposition is trying to accomplish on the power play is key.

You should always utilize hard focus on the puck carrier and soft focus to determine where the other players are setting up on the ice. You will want to play a little deeper in the crease and wait for the play to develop rather than being overly aggressive. On the power play, the opposition is always looking for the open player to pass the puck to, so you need to be aware of where all the opposing players are on the ice. Use soft focus to take a quick look and determine how the opposition is positioned.

When on the power play, the opposition's intention is to get the puck moving east to west in an attempt to get you moving laterally. You want to play a little deeper; it is easier to move laterally because there are no opposing players or teammates to impede your movements. You can get into position quicker and more often as the puck travels around in your own end. You need to be aware of the backdoor player and be ready to either butterfly slide or move across on your feet and butterfly when you get to the destination should a pass go to that player. Whether you butterfly slide or move across while remaining on your feet is dependent on where the opposition player is situated. You need to be aware of the backdoor player so you can make a read on the play and determine the best way to get across in time to make the save. You will also want to determine which hand the open player shoots with so you can defend the pending shot accordingly. If the opposing player is far enough out that you can get across and remain on your feet, then that is the best option for you. However, if the player is positioned closer to the net, you are better off to butterfly slide across so that you are in a save position when you arrive at your destination. If the player receives a pass and takes a one-timer (a shot without first stopping the puck), you will need to butterfly slide across to get there on time to make the save.

At any point in a game, you need to be in control of your rebounds. Because of the shorthanded situation, rebound control becomes even more vital. The same tactics for odd-man rushes discussed earlier in this chapter come into fruition when defending the power play. At the higher levels of hockey, opposition power plays are broken down in the film room prior to the game. This option may not be available for goaltenders at lower levels of hockey, so they must do a fast read on how the opposition power play is set up.

### Goaltender Tips: Defending a Power Play

- If possible before the game, scout the opposition's power play.
- Awareness of how the players are positioned and where the puck is located is key for you in defending a shorthanded situation.
- Be patient and let the play develop in front of you. Don't be overly aggressive.

When on the power play, your ability to play the puck can have a large impact on your team's success. When your team has the extra skater, you can play the puck up ice so your teammates can keep the opposition hemmed into their own end, and in turn, create more scoring opportunities. If you constantly wait for your defenseman to come back and pick up the puck, valuable seconds on the power play will tick away. You can support the power play in the following ways:

- Watch the opposition's bench because if the opportunity arises, you may be able to play the puck up ice and catch them off guard during a line change.

- Keep an eye on the penalty box. Often, at the expiration of a penalty, the unaccounted-for player is sprung loose on a breakaway as he gets on the ice from the penalty box. It is important for you to bang your stick on the ice to signify the end of the penalty to your teammates so they can watch for the player coming out of the penalty box. Do not do this if the other team has control of the puck in your end when the penalty expires.

- Some goaltenders tend to relax while their team has the man advantage, thinking the play will stay in the opposition end. However, blocked shots by the opposition can lead to a quick turnover and odd-man rush against you, and you must be ready to make the save.

- If the opposition clears the puck down the ice, come out of your net and play it up to a teammate if that option is available. If your defenseman would rather you simply leave the puck for him, he needs to communicate that to you.

### Goaltender Tips: Defending Penalty Shots

- Focus on calming your body. Take a couple of deep breaths to settle yourself down.
- Be aware of the way the shooter typically shoots and what side of the ice the shooter is approaching from.
- Be extra patient on the penalty shot.
- Don't be overly aggressive; let the play come to you.
- Follow the puck with your stick.

# SCREENS

When you find yourself facing a screen that is a mix of opposition and defensive players in front of the net that impedes your vision, it is important that you establish your position at the top of the crease early.

The key is to create space between you and the screening forward so you can properly execute and recover. Use the hand opposite the side from which you are looking to hold off the player who is screening. Create your space. For example, if you are looking to your glove side, hold off the opposition with your blocker (figure 6.3) and vice versa. When there is no risk of a shot, it is good if you can pull up out of your stance to locate the puck when there are opposing players in front.

**Figure 6.3** The goaltender holds off opponent with his blocker and looks around the screen.

On a screen, look to the shooter's stick side as often as possible as long as that is the best viewpoint to locate the puck. If you can't find the puck, look around the other side of the screen. It is best to look around the screen, not over or under it. There are situations when a shot is coming from the point, where you may look over the screen if you are in a tall stance. By looking around the screen, you have a better chance of finding the location of the puck while still maintaining maximum net coverage. Don't pull yourself out of the middle of the net to see the puck. Don't look under the screen; use your upper body to look around it. Sometimes, you will lose track of the location of the puck and will have to hurry to find it.

Remember, it may not always be a clean or deflected shot that you have to react to. Often, the opposition player providing the screen actually blocks the shot. It will be easy for you to lose site of the puck since it will land in front of the opposing player. In this instance, the opponent will try to pull you to one side, so you must be prepared to move laterally in your butterfly to follow the play.

# TIP SHOTS AND DEFLECTIONS

Teams practice set plays where the player with the puck shoots it directly at the stick blade of his teammate (who is positioned directly in front of the net) with the intention that he deflects the puck into the net. On a predetermined shot or pass, be aware of the player's stick positioning. When the shot comes in, drop into the puck and the opposition's stick blade at the same time. It is important that you meet the puck at the point of the deflection and collapse your body over it. Some deflections occur from farther out. On unpredictable deflections, you may be required to make a quick, extended save. If a deflection is farther out, it is important to hold your position and not back into the net, watching the puck closely as it deflects off the stick, to give you the best chance to react to the deflection.

# SCRAMBLES

Scramble plays occur when there is heavy traffic around the net and a puck is loose in front. These conditions can create havoc for you. The key to success in these situations is to be as patient as long as possible. Remain down in the butterfly and wait out the battle as it ensues in front. If you see the puck in the crease, don't dive to try to get it. If you miss the puck, it could result in a tap-in goal for the opposition. Choose net coverage by blocking the lower portion of the net in your butterfly instead of diving around the crease to find the puck. The longer you can wait out the play, the more chance you have for success.

When defending a scramble situation, you want to take a lower position while keeping your upper body over the puck. You want to stay physically strong and not get pushed around in a scramble situation because it can become quite a battle between you and the opposition.

# PLAYS OFF THE RUSH

There are so many variations of offensive attacks that you need to be prepared for. The opposition attack is nonstatic. The players are coming at you, and you need to prepare yourself as the play develops in front of you. You need to have laser-like focus on the play coming off the rush and be prepared to defend it. Following, we discuss the most common plays that occur off the opposition rush and some techniques on how to defend them.

## One-on-One

In a one-on-one situation, the opposing forward has two options. He can either shoot or try to go around the defenseman. Often, the opposing forward will try to use your defenseman as a screen and then shoot the puck with the intention of catching you off guard while your vision on the puck is impaired. If the opposition forward beats the defenseman wide, a breakaway situation will occur, and you will utilize the tactics discussed previously. Here are a few other key points for you in a one-on-one situation:

- Be aware of the shooter's options. Is he going to pull wide or shoot straight on through the screen?
- Don't let up. Often, the goaltender will think a shot won't take place because the defenseman has the play covered. You can be beaten with an unexpected shot.
- Make sure you have enough backward momentum in case the shooter pulls you across the crease.
- Make sure you maintain good gap control and do not get caught flat-footed.

## Two-on-One

For many years, it was taught that when facing a two-on-one, the defenseman should take away the pass and leave the shot for the goaltender. With goaltenders now able to move post to post with much more efficiency, this coaching tactic is not always applicable. If facing a two-on-one, the opposing player coming down the wing has three options: he can shoot to score, shoot it off the goaltender to create a rebound, or pass it to his teammate.

You need to have discussions with your defenseman in practice about how you are going to position yourselves on a two-on-one. Is the defenseman going to play more in the middle or to the puck carrier's side? You should play slightly stronger to the puck carrier's side but be ready to play the pass (figure 6.4). Some coaches prefer their defenseman to play strong to the puck

Figure 6.4   Two-on-one: The goaltender plays slightly stronger to the shooter's side.

carrier, whereas others prefer the defenseman to play more toward the middle of the ice. There are still those who prefer the defenseman to take away the pass. As a goaltender, the coaching tactic chosen is out of your control. You need to hold your ground and be aware of the nonpuck carrier's position. If the nonpuck carrier is heading back door, then be ready to butterfly slide and take away the pass play. If the puck carrier shoots far side, you are already in a good position to make the save. If the opposition forward shoots far side, activate your stick to make the save. Here are a few other key points for you in a two-on-one situation:

- Maintain your angle on the shooter. If there is a pass option, play a little deeper in your net in preparation for a butterfly slide.
- Gauge the speed of the opposition skaters early. Know which hand the shooters are.
- Be ready to activate your stick on far-side shots to eliminate any potential rebound.

## Two-on-None

The two-on-none is like the two-on-one except that without a defenseman to apply pressure, the opposition can develop the play much slower. You should prepare for multiple passes back and forth. The objective of the opposing players is to get you moving back and forth with multiple passes and then finish with a good shot for the goal. To defend multiple passes, you may be required to go from a butterfly slide into an inside-edge push into an extended save. You will need to play deeper in your net. The faster a play develops, the deeper you need to be in your net.

Here are a few other key points for you in a two-on-none situation:

- Be patient.
- Stay on your feet as long as possible. If the multiple passes occur far enough out that you can beat them while staying on your feet, then do so. Otherwise, drop into a butterfly and inside-edge push across.
- Read which hand both players shoot with.

## Three-on-Two

When a three-on-two play develops, it is important for you to hold position at the top of the crease. You have more people to be aware of (three opposing players) and how they are layered. The layering of the opposition forwards determines how patient you need to be and how much depth you need in your net. If the opponents are far and spread out, you need to be able to push out and hold the top of your crease. If one player is going hard to the net and the pass comes across, you will need to butterfly slide to make the save.

Since a three-on-two is a slower-developing play than the two-on-one, you can beat the pass by staying on your feet. Communication with your defenseman is key: "I got shot, I got shot."

You have no control over who is going to take the shot. How the defenseman reacts to the play dictates who will shoot the puck. All you can do is control the outcome of the play you face. It is important to give yourself the best chance of making a save by covering the middle of the net. Always be aware of your positioning and surroundings and where the puck is.

Here are a few other key points for you in a three-on-two situation:

- Stay with the puck carrier; hold the top of the paint as long as you can.
- Utilize soft focus to determine where the opposition players are positioned.
- The options for the opposition on a three-on-two are endless, so be patient when the opposing shooter has time and many options with the puck.

# TACTIC DRILLS

The following drills incorporate everything discussed in this chapter: breakaways, odd-man rushes, screens, tips and deflections, and combination scramble plays. Many of the drills can be performed with a variety of players stationed at different positions on the ice to accommodate various types of scrambles, tips, and deflections. As in previous drills, it is important that you pay close attention to detail and form.

Remember, there are endless variables that can occur during a game, so tactic drills need to have gray areas built in to accommodate the diversity of situations. Goaltenders must treat each drill as if it were a gamelike situation. Drills that don't have gray areas are predictable, and the goaltender must refrain from just going through the motions; otherwise, he will not improve his game. Be in the moment and aware of what is happening as it takes place.

The following are some questions a goaltender should ask himself when performing drills:

- Are you aware of which hand opposing players shoot with?
- Are you applying soft and hard focus?
- Are you conscious of your angles and crease positioning?
- Are you watching the puck through screens or just hoping it hits you?
- Are you patient in scramble drills and waiting for the play to come to you?

# Short Breakaway

## Purpose

This drill involves stopping in tight breakaways.

## Setup

The goaltender starts in a set position at the post. Two shooters are situated beside the net with three shooters in front.

## Instructions

1. Shooter A passes the puck out to shooter C, D, or E in front of the net. At the same time, the goaltender follows the pass and moves to the top of the crease.
2. Shooters C, D, and E perform in tight breakaway, attempting to deke the goalie while the goaltender steps back and generates momentum.
3. Shooters C, D, and E attempt to score, and the goaltender butterfly slides to follow the shooter to either side.
4. Repeat the drill, starting with shooter B passing out to C, D, or E.

## Coaching Tips

- Try to make a read on where the shooter beside the net is going to pass the puck. Check the angle of his blade to determine his most likely pass destination.
- Use a powerful, explosive push and stop to get into position.
- Release backward and follow the shooter across the crease.
- Be patient.
- Stay intact for as long as possible, with your head and stick following the puck.

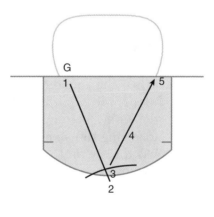

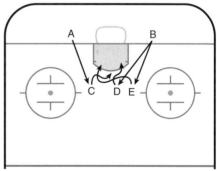

# Three-Puck Breakaway Drill

## Purpose

This drill involves stopping breakaways that initiate from three different locations on the ice. The goaltender must be ready to stop either a shot or a deke.

## Setup

Goaltender starts at the top of the crease facing the shooter to the left. Three shooters are placed along the blue line, each with a puck.

## Instructions

1. Shooter A skates in through the right face-off circle. When he reaches the hash mark, the shooter can either shoot from that position or continue in and deke the goaltender.

2. When the shooter reaches the hash mark and shoots, the goaltender drops into a butterfly and makes the save. If the shooter decides to deke, the goaltender must have enough momentum to butterfly slide, following the shooter across the crease to make the save.

3. The goaltender starts at the top center of his crease facing the shooter in the middle of the ice. Shooter B skates in from the center of the blue line. When he reaches the hash mark, the shooter can either shoot from that position or continue in and deke to either side of the goaltender.

4. When the shooter reaches the hash mark and shoots, the goaltender drops into a butterfly and makes the save. If the shooter decides to deke, the goaltender must have enough momentum to butterfly slide, following the shooter across the crease to make the save. Shooter B has the option to deke to either side, so the goaltender must be ready to move in either direction.

5. The goaltender starts at the top of his crease facing the shooter to the goaltender's right-hand side. Shooter C skates in through the left face-off circle. When he reaches the hash mark, the shooter can either shoot from that position or continue in and deke the goaltender.

6. When the shooter reaches the hash mark and shoots, the goaltender drops into a butterfly and makes the save. If the shooter decides to deke, the goaltender must have enough momentum to butterfly slide, following the shooter across the crease to make the save.

## Coaching Tips

- It is important when facing a breakaway that you hold the middle of your net. Hold your ground and back straight in toward the center of your net.
- You must always control the gap between yourself and the shooter.
- If the shooter pulls you across, follow, keeping your stick aligned to the puck. Make sure you generate enough momentum to follow the shooter across.
- Step out to face the shooter, and then allow your momentum to let you drift back. There are no hard C-cuts either forward or backward.
- This drill can be performed with one shooter or three. If done with one shooter, he simply skates back to the blue line and picks up the second puck and so on.

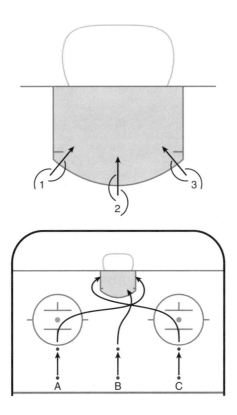

# Double Screen

## Purpose

This drill involves making saves through traffic and players screening.

## Setup

The goaltender starts on the post. Shooters are set up with one shooter on the half wall and another shooter at the top of each of the face-off circles. Two more shooters are positioned in front of the goaltender, creating a screen.

## Instructions

1. Shooter A passes the puck to shooter B. At the same time, the goaltender, starting from his post (G1), steps out and off the post and moves to the top of the crease (G2).

2. Shooter B passes to shooter C. At the same time, the goaltender makes sure to beat the pass and handles the play as a screen with no shot (G3).

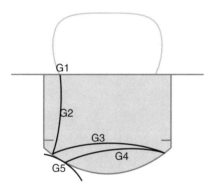

3. Shooter C passes back to shooter B. At the same time, the goaltender makes sure to beat the pass (G4).

4. Shooter B fires a shot through the screen, and the goaltender handles the shot (G5).

## Coaching Tips

- Make sure you beat the pass in both directions.
- Hold off the screen and create space.
- Always try to keep your eye on the puck through the screen. If you do lose it momentarily, try to find it again right away.
- Follow through on the play, meaning once the save has been made, corral and cover or follow any rebounds.

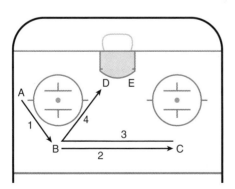

# Shot Pass Drill

## Purpose

This drill involves beating passes and stopping tips and deflections from in tight.

## Setup

The goaltender starts at the post facing the shooter at the half wall. Four shooters are used for this drill. Shooter A is at the half wall. Shooters B and C are situated at opposite sides, just inside the blue line, and shooter D is placed in front of the goaltender.

## Instructions

1. Shooter A passes to shooter B. At the same time, the goaltender, starting from the post (G1), moves out to the top of the crease (G2).

2. Shooter B passes to shooter C. At the same time, the goaltender moves across, making sure to beat the pass (G3).

3. Shooter C passes back to shooter B, and the goaltender follows the pass (G4).

4. Shooter B takes a shot pass to shooter D, while the goaltender recognizes the puck is going to shooter D in front (G5).

5. Shooter D attempts to tip the puck past the goaltender, and the goaltender drops into the butterfly to make the save (G6).

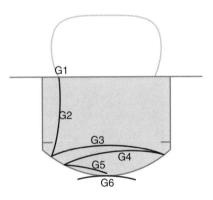

## Coaching Tips

- Work hard to beat the pass every time.
- Use soft focus to see where the players are situated on the ice.
- Be aware of shooter D's stick placement. Drop into the puck and stick to make the save.
- The drill can be made more intricate by having the shooter move to slightly different positions, for example, back door.

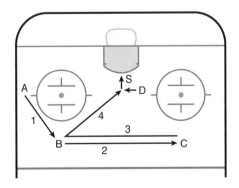

# Pass-In-Front Scramble

## Purpose

This drill involves stopping scramble plays in tight.

## Setup

The goaltender starts at the top of the blue paint in the center of the crease. Two shooters are required for this drill. Shooter A is placed just inside the blue line in the center. Shooter B is placed just outside the goaltender's crease.

## Instructions

1. Shooter A passes the puck to shooter B.
2. Shooter B dekes the goaltender and tries to score.
3. The goaltender plays the deke to either side. The drill is not complete until there is either a goal or the puck is covered up.

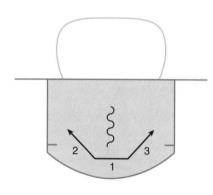

## Coaching Tips

- This drill is slightly abstract, so it is best to perform the drill both ways. Require goalies to stay on their feet as long as possible and then go down and battle. Then, on the next repetition, have them drop into the butterfly as soon as the hard pass is sent to shooter B and battle from the knees.
- Play the drill out until completion.

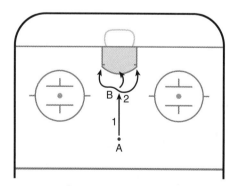

# Pass-In-Front Scramble With Screen

## Purpose

This drill involves scramble plays in front while fighting through a screen.

## Setup

The goaltender starts at the top center of the crease. Three shooters are required for this drill. Shooter A is situated just inside the blue line. Shooters B and C are in front of the goaltender.

## Instructions

1. Shooter A passes the puck in to shooter B.
2. Shooter B plays the puck on a deke to either side.
3. Shooter C stands in front of the goalie and is very passive. His sole purpose is to add more clutter in front of the net.
4. The goaltender looks around the screen and plays the deke to either side. The drill is not complete until there is either a goal or the puck is covered up.

## Coaching Tips

- All players must be engaged in the battle.
- Keep your head over the puck and be prepared to move either way.
- Keep the stick aligned with the puck.
- Try not to open up and scramble too early.

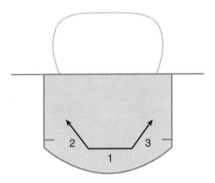

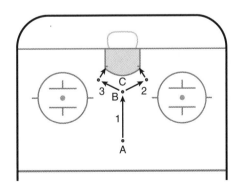

# Chapter 7
# Off-Ice Training

## Maria Mountain

The ability to perform all of the on-ice tactics discussed in the book to this point are what separate the elite goalies from the mediocre. But what about off-ice preparation? How should a goaltender train in the gym in order to be the best possible on-ice athlete he can be? Physical fitness is a year-round program for elite athletes.

In this chapter, we focus on mobility, speed, agility and stamina training for goaltenders. The chapter is chalk full of routines and exercises to help with your physical conditioning to increase your efficiency in movements and stamina when you are in the net.

Off-ice training provides the tools goaltenders need to perform their movements required on the ice quickly and skillfully. Your off-ice training will include stretching (flexibility and mobility training) to reduce wear and tear on your joints and to get your body into position for a save; picture a goaltender with a wide butterfly flare who can take away the bottom of the net. You need stability training that targets not just the torso, or core, but also teaches you to stabilize through different movement patterns using the hips, torso, and upper body.

Strength training provides the building blocks for speed and power by giving you the ability to produce more force. Power and speed training teaches you how to apply the right amount of force in the right direction so you can move with agility and precision on the ice.

The final piece of the puzzle is stamina training so you can continue to move with speed and precision for an entire game and into overtime if necessary. All the pieces—flexibility, mobility, stability, strength, speed, and stamina—fit together to build a complete goaltender.

# Workout Terminology Review

As you engage in workouts or build your own programs, you'll encounter terms that are used to set the parameters of the workout. Most of these terms are familiar to you, but let's review them before we move on.

## Reps

A rep is one complete cycle of an exercise from starting position, to midpoint, to the finish position. For example, if you do one push-up, you have done one rep. If you do 10 push-ups, you have done 10 reps.

## Sets

A collection of reps is one set. For example, doing 10 push-ups equals one set of 10 reps.

## Tempo

The tempo for each exercise is given as four numbers representing the different phases of the exercise: lowering phase, pause at the bottom, lifting phase, and pause at the top. A tempo of 3-0-1-1, for example, means you will lower the resistance for three seconds, pause for zero seconds at the bottom of the movement, lift the resistance for one second, and pause for one second at the top. For example, applying this to the push-up would mean that you would lower your chest to the floor over three seconds and without any pause at the bottom, push up to the top of the movement over a count of one and pause at the top of the push-up for one second. It is essential that you follow the tempo provided for each exercise because the tempo determines the time your muscles are under tension and whether you are training them for stability, strength, or power.

## Supersets

In some of the workouts that follow, you will see "supersets," or collections of exercises that go together. You will complete all sets of all exercises within a superset before moving on. For example, if you see a superset consisting of dumbbell squat lateral and push-ups, you will complete one set of eight reps each way of the dumbbell squat lateral followed by one set of 12 push-ups. That is one superset; then, you will complete two more supersets for a total of three sets before moving on.

# FLEXIBILITY AND MOBILITY TRAINING

Have you noticed that the flexibility you get when you are stretching at home is not there once you step on the ice? This happens because you are lacking the functional range of motion every goaltender needs; your body is trying to protect you by keeping you out of positions you cannot stabilize.

In the section that follows, you will discover different ways of stretching that are based on the work of Dr. Andreo Spina, a movement pattern specialist who helps athletes maximize performance and recover from injury. You will learn how to stretch and generate tension, which is what gives you the type of flexibility you can use on the ice. It is referred to as "mobility," which is stretching plus stability. It teaches your body that it can generate high levels of force and stabilize itself in extended and potentially vulnerable positions.

## Types of Flexibility and Mobility Training

Most goaltenders are familiar with static stretching to improve hip flexibility. It is one piece of the puzzle, but there are other methods that also help you not only achieve flexible hips, but also stable hips. Here, you will discover the difference between static and dynamic stretching, see how self-myofascial release improves range of motion, and discover how the dynamic warm-up ties it all together.

### Dynamic and Static Stretching

Sitting on the floor in front of the TV and stretching will increase your passive range of motion, but not your functional range of motion. Passive range of motion describes the flexibility you have when you stretch just your groin muscles while sitting on the floor or working on your splits at home. It is specific to the joint angle you are stretching and can be assisted using your body weight.

Functional range of motion is dynamic flexibility. It requires the coordination of flexibility and stability in different segments of the body. Let's say you are in your butterfly and you need to kick your left leg out to make a second save. You will need to use your core muscles to stabilize your torso as you rapidly extend the left leg, putting a huge stretch on the groin muscles and hamstrings. Your muscles must be smart enough and strong enough to control the muscle during that rapid stretch. You do not develop those qualities with regular static stretches.

In lab testing of the vertical jump and maximum weight lifting, there was a slight decrease in peak strength and power production following static stretching; therefore, some believe that static stretching makes an athlete weak. Follow-up research, on the contrary, showed that this loss in power is mitigated when followed by dynamic stretching. Dynamic stretching is what you see many pro goaltenders performing as part of their off-ice warm-up (i.e., walking lunges, high kicks, or lateral shuffles).

Much like strength training, stretching has risks. In fact, all forms of training have an element of risk, but the benefits of improved hip flexibility and a wider butterfly flare and the ability to make an occasional toe save outweigh the risks. It is still a valuable training tool when used with the right volume and intensity to minimize your risk and maximize your returns. That's why goaltenders still use static stretching.

## Dynamic Warm-Ups

One of the most effective things goaltenders can do to increase their probability of success on the ice is to perform a proper dynamic warm-up off the ice. The on-ice warm-up is often about warming up the shooters, which doesn't leave much time for your warm-up. You don't want to spend the first few minutes of a game or practice getting warmed up. Instead, set yourself up for success even before you step on the ice.

A warm-up mitigates the decrease in peak power that we see after static stretching. It also activates your neuromuscular and energy systems so you are ready to do your multidirectional work. As you warm up, be mindful of what the purpose of each movement is and what you are trying to accomplish.

## Self-Myofascial Release

Self-myofascial release is a form of self-massage. Some people argue that self-myofascial release, such as foam rolling, does nothing but increase your tolerance to foam rolling. In other words, it might feel uncomfortable in the beginning, but the more you do it, the better it feels. The argument is that it does not change the tissue quality; rather, it changes just the tolerance to that activity. Let's look at some compelling evidence to show how self-myofascial release impacts your flexibility.

Here's an experiment that will demonstrate the effect of self-myofascial release:

Take off your shoes, and get a tennis ball, lacrosse ball, squash ball, golf ball, or whatever type of small ball you have nearby. Stand with your feet side by side and your knees perfectly straight; then bend forward as if you're trying to touch your toes, and make a mental note of how far you can get. Can you get your fingertips midway down your shin? Can you get your fingertips to the floor? Can you place your palms flat on the floor? Continue standing, and for 60 seconds on each foot, roll the ball over the bottom of your

# Precautions for Stretching

When you have an actual impingement, you should not be trying to increase your range of motion. Don't panic. I know the word "impingement" has you visualizing surgery, but there are many reasons for impingement and not all of them require surgery to correct. There could be a restriction from the connective tissue in your hip, called capsular tightness; an issue with the positioning of the ball in the socket that limits your range of motion; or a true, bony impingement.

If you're doing a stretch and feeling a block, or pinch, on the closing side of the joint rather than a nice stretch in the muscle on the opening side of the joint, you should proceed with caution. For example, let's look at the hamstring stretch. As you pivot forward at the hips to feel a stretch in the back of your thigh, which is the opening side of the joint (the area you are trying to stretch), if you are feeling a pinch (or block) in the front of your hip, which is the closing side of the joint, then do not try to force that range of motion. Rather, you should get it assessed by a sport physiotherapist or other health care provider who has experience assessing athletes. He or she will be able to help determine the cause of that block, or pinch, and create a plan to overcome it.

As a goaltender, you want to focus on stretching movements more than stretching isolated muscles. As an example, your adductors, or groin muscles, work with your oblique abdominals. In other words, the muscles of your inner thigh and hip work with the muscles running diagonally across your torso. That complete chain must be mobile. Although most goaltenders spend a lot of effort stretching out their groin muscles, trying to get the elusive splits, they ignore their oblique abdominals. This creates a weak link in the chain and contributes to lower abdominal strains, groin strains, and sports hernias.

To summarize, when you stretch, it is OK to feel a stretching sensation in the muscle you are targeting, but you should not feel pinching or pain in the joint. Do not continue to force your stretches if you experience the discomfort or blocking sensation described above.

foot, from the base of your heel to the base of your toes. Exert some body weight on to the ball with enough pressure that it feels mildly uncomfortable, but not painful. Once you've done 60 seconds on each side, repeat the test. Stand with your feet touching and knees locked straight, and bend forward at the hips. How far do you get now? Typically, you will see an increase of two to six inches after doing this self-myofascial release technique. This gives you a clear demonstration of how self-myofascial release can improve your flexibility. When you include it in your mobility training, here are some things to keep in mind:

- Go slowly. Think of it as a massage, not a ride at an amusement park.

- Feel and familiarize yourself with the quality of your tissue. Does it feel smooth, are there knots, is a specific muscle more sensitive today than it was yesterday, or is there a difference between sides?

- Scour the muscle by rolling the lacrosse ball or foam roller over all surfaces of the target muscle. Find the tender spots and trigger points; then hold constant pressure on them until the tension in that area dissipates.

## Mobility Training Programs

Here, you will find two sample mobility programs to improve movement (see tables 7.1 and 7.2). While it is fine to alternate between the mobility routines, do not substitute exercises from one program to the other. Use a lacrosse or tennis ball for your routine.

Complete your daily mobility routine either as a stand-alone workout or before your dynamic warm-up or off-ice workout. Once per day, five days per week is a good goal, but you can do your stretching as much as twice per day, seven days per week. Just remember that you are not trying to force your stretches; it takes time to improve mobility, so consistency is the key.

Also, think about what you're stretching and feel it as you go. Make it mindful. By mindful, we mean being in the moment and thinking only about the stretch you are performing. See how it carries over onto the ice. It shouldn't be a task where you just sit and do your stretches. Think of it as mobility training, just as you would when you're working out in the gym.

Goaltenders should warm up before they train both on and off the ice. Table 7.3 is a dynamic warm-up to use before off-ice training sessions, and table 7.4 is a dynamic warm-up to use before stepping on the ice, which progresses from self-myofascial release to increase blood flow to the muscle and let you explore how your muscles are feeling in terms of knots or tight spots,

### Table 7.1   Daily Mobility Program 1

| Exercise | Sets | Reps/duration | Page numbers |
|---|---|---|---|
| Ball on hip flexor | Perform one set of each exercise. Start with ball on hip flexor and finish with active dorsiflexion. | 30 sec each side | 145 |
| Ball on glutes | | 30 sec each side | 146 |
| Ball on foot | | 30 sec each side | 147 |
| Half-kneeling groin stretch with rock back | | 10 each side | 149 |
| Hip flexor stretch with foot on wall | | 30 sec each side | 150 |
| Lat stretch with hands on foam roll | | 4 breaths | 151 |
| Active dorsiflexion | | 15 each side | 152 |

## Table 7.2  Daily Mobility Program 2

| Exercise | Sets | Reps/duration | Page numbers |
|---|---|---|---|
| Ball on hip flexor | Perform one set of each exercise. Start with ball on hip flexor and finish with butterfly flow. | 30 sec each side | 145 |
| Ball on glutes | | 30 sec each side | 146 |
| Ball on adductor | | 30 sec each side | 147 |
| Ball on foot | | 30 sec each side | 148 |
| Figure-four stretch | | 30 sec each side | 153 |
| Elevated hamstring stretch with active rotation | | 15 each side | 154 |
| Hip flexor stretch with foot on wall | | 30 sec each side | 150 |
| Quadruped rock back with T-spine rotation | | 5 each side | 155 |
| Butterfly flow | | 2 each direction | 156 |

## Table 7.3  Off-Ice Training Warm-Up

| Exercise | Sets | Reps/duration | Page numbers |
|---|---|---|---|
| Walking quad stretch | Perform one set of each exercise. Start with walking quad stretch and finish with wall juggle with hip shift. | 4 each side | 157 |
| Walking knee hug | | 4 each side | 158 |
| Hip shift down and back | | 4 each side | 159 |
| Inverted reach | | 4 each side | 160 |
| Sumo squat to pop | | 4 each side | 161 |
| Lateral shuffle to deceleration | | 4 each side | 162 |
| Wall juggle with hip shift | | 60 sec | 163 |

## Table 7.4  On-Ice Training Warm-Up

| Exercise | Sets | Reps/duration | Page numbers |
|---|---|---|---|
| Ball on glutes | Perform one set of each exercise. Start with ball on glutes and finish with wall juggle with hip shift. | 30 sec each side | 146 |
| Ball on hip flexor | | 30 sec each side | 145 |
| Hip flexor stretch with foot on wall | | 30 sec each side | 150 |
| Elevated hamstring stretch with active rotation | | 15 each side | 154 |
| Active dorsiflexion | | 15 each side | 152 |
| Half-kneeling groin stretch with rock back | | 15 each side | 149 |
| Quadruped rock back with T-spine rotation | | 5 each side | 155 |
| Walking quad stretch | | 4 each side | 157 |
| Walking knee hug | | 4 each side | 158 |
| Hip shift down and back | | 4 each side | 159 |
| Inverted reach | | 4 each side | 160 |
| Sumo squat to pop | | 4 each way | 167 |
| Lateral shuffle to deceleration | | 4 each side | 162 |
| Wall juggle with hip shift | | 60 sec | 163 |

to static stretching, which will give you another opportunity to see how your muscles are feeling and increase your range of motion.

To get you ready to stop pucks, move on to the dynamic warm-up drills, finishing with eye-hand coordination and nervous system activation, which prime your senses and activate some of the motor pathways you will rely on for tracking the puck and making saves.

Again, make sure you are doing each exercise properly and pay attention to where you feel the stretch because if you are not doing the warm-up exercises properly, then you're not warming up the areas that reduce your risk of injury and improve your performance.

## Mobility Training Exercises

This section includes the exercises listed in the daily mobility training programs (tables 7.1–7.4). Read through each exercise description thoroughly as you go through the workouts. Pay attention to how your muscles feel with each movement.

# Ball on Hip Flexor

## Purpose

This is a soft-tissue release technique that unlocks flexibility in the hip flexors, allowing you to have a longer stride and reduce your risk of hip-flexor strains.

## Setup

Sit on the floor with your legs straight out in front of you. Lay your thumb across the crease in the front of one of your hips and lift that straight leg up two to three inches off the floor. Feel that bundle of muscle? This is where you will focus.

## Instructions

1. Place the ball over the thick bundle of muscle in the front of your hip and roll to your stomach so the ball is sandwiched between the floor and your hip.
2. Slowly and methodically move your body over the ball as you explore all aspects of the muscle. Stay off any bony prominences and your abdominal area.
3. If you find a tender spot, or trigger point, stay on that spot, and apply pressure until the trigger point dissipates; then continue.

## Coaching Tips

- Go slowly.
- Try to feel the difference in tissue quality throughout the muscle.
- Relax the muscle you are working on.

# Ball on Glutes

## Purpose

This is a soft-tissue release technique that unlocks flexibility in the glutes, allowing you to access more range of motion in your hips.

## Setup

Sit on the floor with the ball under one of your buttocks.

## Instructions

1. Place the ball under the thick, muscular portion of your glutes. You can use your feet and hands to unload some of the pressure on the ball if it is uncomfortable.
2. Slowly and methodically move your body over the ball as you roll from the midline of your buttock outward toward the hip.
3. If you find a tender spot, or trigger point, stay on that spot, and apply pressure until the trigger point dissipates; then continue.

## Coaching Tips

- Go slowly.
- Try to feel the difference in tissue quality throughout the muscle.
- Relax the muscle you are working on.

# Ball on Adductor

## Purpose

This is a soft-tissue release technique that unlocks flexibility in the adductors (groin muscles), allowing you to access more range of motion in your hip and get deeper splits.

## Setup

Sit on the floor in a hurdler stretch position, and place the ball under the thick muscular portion of the adductor of your bent leg.

## Instructions

1. Slowly and methodically move your leg over the ball as you roll along the length of the muscle. Split the adductor into thirds, starting with the third closest to the knee and then working your way up. For some of you, it might be tricky to get up high into your groin from the floor position. If so, switch to a foam roll; it will give you more room to work.

2. If you find a tender spot, or trigger point, stay on that spot, and apply pressure until the trigger point dissipates; then continue.

## Coaching Tips

- Go slowly.
- Try to feel the difference in tissue quality throughout the muscle.
- Relax the muscle you are working on.
- Rotate your thigh to get the front and back portion of your adductors.

# Ball on Foot

## Purpose

This is a soft-tissue release technique that unlocks flexibility in the calves, hamstrings, glutes, and back extensors.

## Setup

Remove your shoes and place the ball under one foot.

## Instructions

1. Press your foot onto the ball, creating enough pressure that it feels mildly uncomfortable, but not painful.
2. Slowly and methodically roll the ball over all aspects of the bottom of your foot, from the base of your heel to the base of your toes.
3. If you find a tender spot, or trigger point, stay on that spot, and apply pressure until the trigger point dissipates; then continue.

## Coaching Tips

- Go slowly.
- Try to feel the difference in tissue quality throughout the bottom of your foot.

# Half-Kneeling Groin Stretch With Rock Back

## Purpose

This is a dynamic stretch that targets different portions of your adductors (groin muscles).

## Setup

Kneel on all fours. With one knee directly under your hip, extend the other leg straight out to the side.

## Instructions

1. Make sure your lower back is not rounded.
2. Reach your extended leg out until you feel a medium to strong stretch in your adductors.
3. Without changing your back position, rock your hips straight back to feel the stretch deepen.
4. Pause and then return to the starting position.

## Coaching Tips

- Go slowly.
- Use a mirror to watch your back position. Do not let it change as you rock back; you are trying to isolate movement at your hip joint only.
- Relax the muscle you are working on.

# Hip Flexor Stretch With Foot on Wall

## Purpose

This is a static stretch technique to lengthen the muscle in the front of your thigh that crosses your hip and knee. It gets tight with sitting and in your ready position, so it needs to be stretched often.

## Setup

Use a dense cushion or high-quality exercise mat to cushion your knee. Position the mat in front of the wall.

## Instructions

1. Face away from the wall with one foot flat on the floor in a half-kneeling position and one foot on the wall.
2. Slowly lift your torso until you feel a medium to strong stretch in the front of your hip and thigh. Do not hyperextend your back by trying to get your torso all the way upright.

### Coaching Tips

- Slowly come up from the starting position.
- Stop when you feel a stretch in the front of your thigh. Going farther will extend your lower back.
- If you want to feel more stretch, try to tuck your buttocks under or squeeze your glutes.

# Lat Stretch With Hands on Foam Roll

## Purpose

This is a stretch for your midback muscles, with an emphasis on expansion of the rib cage to improve thoracic spine mobility and let you stay big in the net.

## Setup

Kneel on the floor with your arms outstretched and wrists on a foam roll.

## Instructions

1. Rock back on your hips as far as you comfortably can (or until your buttocks are at your heels).
2. Reach through your arms, trying to lengthen the distance from your fingertips to your buttocks.
3. Breathe in through your nose for four seconds; exhale through your mouth for six seconds.

## Coaching Tip

- As you breathe, focus on expanding your rib cage fully on the inspiration and exhaling all your air on the exhalation.

# Active Dorsiflexion

## Purpose

This is a dynamic stretch that helps you get more movement at your ankle so you can get into your low ready stance and keep your weight toward the ball of your foot.

## Setup

Stand in front of a wall with both feet pointing straight forward. One foot will be slightly in front of the other. You will perform the exercise with your front foot.

## Instructions

1. Keep your foot pointing straight ahead and your heel on the ground throughout the set.
2. Flex at your ankle, bringing your shin forward over your foot until you feel a gentle stretch or a tightness in the lower third of your calf.

## Coaching Tips

- You might naturally be tempted to turn your foot outward or let your knee fall inward. Try not to do that.
- You will not feel much stretch in the bulk of your calf, just a tightness.

# Figure-Four Stretch

## Purpose

This is a stretch to help open up your hip.

## Setup

Lie on your left side with your right foot just above and in front of your left knee.

## Instructions

1. Roll to your stomach with your knee pointing out to the side.
2. Squeeze your glutes to assist the stretch by moving the hip bone on the stretch side toward the floor.

## Coaching Tip

- This will feel more like a tightness in the front of the hip than a muscular stretch.

# Elevated Hamstring Stretch With Active Rotation

## Purpose

This is a dynamic stretch to target the different portions of your hamstrings.

## Setup

Stand in front of a box or table that is approximately hip height. Place your foot and lower leg on the bench and stand up tall in your torso.

## Instructions

1. Place your hands on your pelvis, and without moving your leg, rotate your pelvis. This is called "pelvis on femur" rotation. Make sure the movement is from the pelvis, not from the shoulders and upper body.

2. Move at a steady, continuous pace.

## Coaching Tips

- As you open up your hip, you will feel the stretch toward your groin.
- As you close your hip, you will feel the stretch toward the outside of your thigh.

# Quadruped Rock Back With T-Spine Rotation

## Purpose

This is a dynamic stretch to improve the movement of your midback. This will let you stay taller in the net and take the load off your lower back.

## Setup

Kneel on all fours. Rock back on your hips, but maintain a straight back position.

## Instructions

1. Place your right hand behind your right ear.
2. Rotate your upper torso and your head toward the right. Your head will rotate along with your torso.
3. Pause at the top and return to the starting position.

## Coaching Tip

- Isolate the movement to your mid and upper torso. Do not rotate your lower back.

# Butterfly Flow

## Purpose

This is a dynamic mobility drill that improves your hip mobility and stability.

## Setup

Sit on the floor with your feet together and knees out to the side (like a butterfly stretch ; see photo *a*).

## Instructions

1. Roll from your sitting position to kneeling position while keeping your torso stable (see photos *a-b*).
2. Slowly roll back to a seated position, moving as slowly as you can with maximum control (see photo *a*).

## Coaching Tip

- Athletes should not jerk with their bodies to get the movements going.

# Walking Quad Stretch

## Purpose

This is a dynamic exercise to stretch the front of your thigh.

## Setup

Start in a tall standing position with both feet pointing forward.

## Instructions

1. Balancing on one leg, bring your heel to your buttock on the other side, grabbing your ankle with your hand.
2. Hold your heel to your buttock to feel a stretch in the front of your thigh.
3. Repeat with the other leg.

## Coaching Tip

- Make sure your knees stay side by side in the stretch position. Do not let the knee on the stretching side get pulled outward.

# Walking Knee Hug

## Purpose

This is a dynamic stretch for your hips and glutes.

## Setup

Start in a tall standing position with both feet pointing forward.

## Instructions

1. Balancing on one leg, use both hands to pull your other knee up toward your chest.
2. Stay tall in your chest. Feel the stretch in your hip.

## Coaching Tip

- Focus on pulling your knee toward your chest rather than dropping your chest toward your knee.

# Hip Shift Down and Back

## Purpose

This is a dynamic stretch to open up your hips and stretch out your groin muscles.

## Setup

Start in a tall standing position with both feet pointing forward. You will be stepping to the side.

## Instructions

1. Step sideways with your right leg, shifting your weight over the right foot.
2. Then, shift back to the left foot, feeling a stretch in each side of the groin as you move side to side.
3. Push off the trailing leg (the left leg) to return to your starting position.

## Coaching Tip

- Take your time to feel a stretch in each side of the groin, and make sure you get a powerful push off the trailing leg.

# Inverted Reach

## Purpose

This is a dynamic stretch for your hamstrings.

## Setup

Start in a tall standing position with both feet pointing forward.

## Instructions

1. Balancing on one leg, pivot forward at the hips, keeping your arms and trailing leg in line with your torso.
2. Pivot forward at the hip until you feel the stretch at the back of the thigh of the leg that is on the floor.
3. Return to the starting position and repeat on the other side.

## Coaching Tip

- Keep your hips flat to the floor. Do not open up with your hips as you pivot forward.

# Sumo Squat to Pop

## Purpose

This is a dynamic stretch for your hips.

## Setup

Start in a tall standing position with both feet pointing forward. You will be stepping to the side.

## Instructions

1. Step sideways, leading with your right leg to a double hip-width stance, and keep your knees wide while squatting down (see photo).
2. From the bottom position, drive off both legs to pop straight up.
3. Land with both feet hip-width apart.
4. Step again with your right foot and repeat.

## Coaching Tips

- As you squat down, actively pull your knees apart.
- Make sure you maintain a neutral back position during the squat portion.

# Lateral Shuffle to Deceleration

## Purpose

This is a dynamic stretch for your adductors and a dynamic deceleration drill.

## Setup

Start in a tall standing position with both feet pointing forward. You will be shuffling to the side.

## Instructions

1. Stay low in the legs throughout. Shuffle two strides to your right; decelerate on your right leg.
2. Push off the right leg, shuffle two strides to your left, and decelerate on the left leg.

## Coaching Tips

- Maintain a neutral back position as you decelerate.
- Use your hip, knee, and ankle on the deceleration side to come to a complete stop.
- Your trailing leg will remain extended, and you should feel a stretch in the groin.

# Wall Juggle With Hip Shift

## Purpose

This is a dynamic eye-hand coordination drill.

## Setup

Stand with feet hip-width apart in front of a wall and hold a ball in each hand. Use a tennis ball, lacrosse ball, or other type of ball that will bounce back to you.

## Instructions

1. Alternate passing and catching the balls off the wall as you continually shift your hips from side to side.
2. Catch the balls in your hand when they rebound off the wall.

## Coaching Tips

- Make sure to shift all the way over your right foot and all the way over your left foot. Continuously keep that rhythm. Do not stop as you juggle the ball.
- Follow the ball into your hand with your eyes to practice your tracking skills.

# STRENGTH TRAINING

Strength is your vehicle to power and speed. You want strong muscles that work together in functional chains to produce explosive, powerful, multiplanar movements. You don't get that type of strength from doing the leg press, the knee extension, the groin machine, or the bench press because machine-based training does not integrate your core into the movement. Consider the leg press versus a single-leg squat: when an athlete does a leg press, the path of the weight is not going to deviate. The load is carried on a fixed path, and there is no need for stabilization.

Also, consider that this type of training does not require dynamic stabilization of the torso because of the fixed seat. Dynamic stabilization is what goaltenders need on the ice to respond to different movements generated by the lower body; the integrated stabilization between your ankles, knees, and hips is what keeps you balanced. Some goaltenders find the leg press to be an attractive training tool. They might be able to front squat 165 pounds before their lower back starts to feel a strain. Naturally, they want to lift more because they want strong legs, so they get on the leg press and find that they can lift 300 pounds. These players are trying to do the right thing. They think, "Wow! I'm really building strength; those squats were holding me back because my low back was limiting the exercise. With the leg press, I am going to have super strong legs."

However, on the ice, you use your torso, hips, knees, and ankles together as a functional unit. If you build legs that are capable of producing 300 pounds of force and they are attached to a torso that has trouble stabilizing 165 pounds of force, you can see that you have accidentally created a weak link in the chain where your torso (or core) cannot support or stabilize the force production capability of your legs. This is where you see minimal change in your actual speed on the ice and get into trouble with back pain and hip and groin injuries.

It's an oversimplification, but I think you can see the difference between building functionally strong muscles that a goalie needs to maneuver on the ice and muscles that are strong in the gym. You will see lots of similarities in the gym between you and your teammates who play forward or defense. You will still squat, push, pull, and rotate just like the skaters do, but you will put more emphasis on frontal-plane movement. Think of pushing from post to post on the ice; that is a frontal-plane movement.

The takeaway here is that a goaltender needs to be strong enough to do his job. For example, if you can front squat 300 pounds with a barbell, don't be too concerned with getting to 350 pounds. Instead, look for a way to make this exercise more challenging in a functional way, like moving to single-leg squats. If you can front squat 300 pounds, you should be able to single-leg squat at least 150 pounds (75-pound dumbbell in each hand). You will see how challenging single-leg squats with dumbbells are compared to the barbell squats. They require more stabilization at the hip, knee, ankle, and torso, thus increasing the functional demand on the torso, hip, knee, and ankle without adding more weight (and more wear and tear) to a basic exercise pattern.

Note that you will also spend more time working on the rotator cuff muscles of your hip. Typically, the term rotator cuff is used to describe the muscles that help stabilize the shoulder joint. I am borrowing the term to describe the muscles that help stabilize and control the hip joint in a similar way. Goalies need to focus on those muscles the same way a baseball pitcher focuses on the shoulder. You will also spend extra time putting your muscles under tension to lengthen them the way you use them on the ice. Goalies and skaters will share many of the same exercises; a goalie-specific program will differ by about 30 percent with specialized training.

## Strength Training Programs

Here are two full-body strength training workouts that improve a goaltender's performance and reduce his risk of injury (see tables 7.5 and 7.6). Pay close attention to performing the movements with quality while sticking to the proper tempos. Complete the workouts with purpose, and focus on the muscles you are working. Going through the motions won't get you maximum benefit. Ask yourself questions like, "Where do I feel this?", and, "How has this movement improved since the last time I did it?". Finally, understand that the purpose of a training program is not to simply make you tired. The purpose here is to show you some foundational strength training exercises that will benefit you; some target your big muscle groups and some develop your smaller stabilizers. You might be wondering where the core work is. It's in there. It's just integrated and functional. Your core never really works unless your arms and legs are working, so that's how we train it.

## Strength Training Exercises

This section includes the exercises listed in the strength training programs (tables 7.5 and 7.6). Maintain good form throughout all of your movements. Being in control of your movements as you work your muscles will provide optimal results. Be conscious of your back position and hips as you proceed through each exercise.

## Table 7.5 Full-Body Strength Training Program 1

| Exercise | | Sets* | Reps | Tempo | Page numbers |
|---|---|---|---|---|---|
| Superset A | A1. Sumo squat | 3 | 12 | 3-0-1-1 | 167 |
| | A2. Tall kneeling bungee press | | 12 | 3-0-1-1 | 168 |
| Superset B | B1. Half-groin oblique row | 2 | 8 each side | 2-0-1-1 | 169 |
| | B2. Half-groin cable lift | | 8 each side | 2-0-1-1 | 170 |
| | B3. Knee recovery lateral hop | | 4 each side | Hold 3 sec | 171 |

*Do not rest between sets. This program is designed to let one body part rest while you are training a different area.

## Table 7.6 Full-Body Strength Training Program 2

| Exercise | | Sets* | Reps | Tempo | Page numbers |
|---|---|---|---|---|---|
| Superset A | A1. Lateral lunge balance | 3 | 6 each side | 10 × 3 | 172 |
| | A2. Half-kneeling bungee pec fly (outside foot forward) | | 8 each side | 1-0-1-2 | 173 |
| Superset B | B1. Push-up and reach | 3 | 4 each side | 2-0-1-1 | 174 |
| | B2. Reverse crease bungee push | | 15 each side | 1-0-1-1 | 175 |
| Superset C | C1. Squat jump and hold | 3 | 6 | 3 jumps + 5-sec hold | 176 |
| | C2. Contra dumbbell row | | 8 each side | 2-0-1-1 | 177 |
| | C3. Three-way medicine ball squeeze | | 1 each side | 15-sec squeeze | 178 |

*Do not rest between sets. This program is designed to let one body part rest while you are training a different area.

# Sumo Squat

## Purpose

This is a lower-body strengthening exercise that lengthens your groin muscles under tension.

## Setup

Stand with feet hip-width apart and hold one dumbbell in each hand just above the shoulders (see photo).

## Instructions

1. Keep your knees over your ankles by actively using your hips to pull your knees apart.
2. Squat down with your hips as far as you comfortably can with neutral back position. Notice a stretch in your groin muscles as you squat down.

## Coaching Tips

- Only go as far as you can without rounding your lower back.
- It is OK to pivot your torso forward from your hips.

# Tall Kneeling Bungee Press

## Purpose

This is an upper-body strength and core stabilization exercise.

## Setup

Kneel on both knees in front of either a resistance band or a cable column.

## Instructions

1. Stay tall in your torso and keep your hips forward. Do not sit back on your buttocks.
2. Maintain this stable torso position as you press the weight forward with both arms.
3. Return to the starting position under control and repeat.

## Coaching Tips

- Focus on engaging your abdominals to stabilize your torso as you press.
- Think about your position in the net when keeping your hips forward.

# Half-Groin Oblique Row

## Purpose

This is an upper-body strength exercise that incorporates the chain of muscles from the adductors to the obliques.

## Setup

Kneel on your right knee with your left leg extended straight out to your side. The resistance will be attached to your right and you will be pulling across your body. You can use a resistance band or cable column.

## Instructions

1. With your right arm, reach across your body and row the cable or resistance band, almost like pulling a bow and arrow.
2. Return to the starting position with control.

## Coaching Tips

- You should feel a stretch in the extended groin.
- Feel how your abdominal muscles engage during the row.

# Half-Groin Cable Lift

## Purpose

This is a dynamic core stabilization exercise incorporating the chain of muscles from your groin through your abdominals.

## Setup

Kneel on your right knee with your left leg extended toward a cable column or resistance band. The cable column or resistance band is on your left.

## Instructions

1. Grab the handle with both hands. Feel a stretch on your extended right groin.
2. Without rotating your torso, lift your arms from low to high with the low point opposite your left hip and the high point opposite your right shoulder. Your arms should stay straight through the entire movement.

## Coaching Tips

- This is a smaller range of motion than you might expect.
- Do not rotate your torso at all. Maintain your core stability.

# Knee Recovery Lateral Hop

## Purpose

This is a lateral power and deceleration exercise.

## Setup

Kneel on both knees with a tall torso.

## Instructions

1. From the tall kneeling position, bring your left foot up and under your body as though you were going to transition from a butterfly with a push to your right while recovering to your skates. Get a full push to your right.
2. Land on your right leg with the hip, knee, and ankle bent; stick the landing.
3. Hold for three seconds; then return to your starting position.

## Coaching Tips

- Make sure you're getting a full push off the outside leg.
- The goal is to stick the landing in a balanced, low ready position.

# Lateral Lunge Balance

## Purpose

This is a dynamic lower-body strength and power exercise requiring deceleration and balance.

## Setup

Stand with feet hip-width apart and hold one dumbbell in each hand at shoulder height.

## Instructions

1. Step to your right, leading with your right leg, and squat down over the right foot so your hip, knee, ankle, and shoulders are stacked.
2. Forcefully push off your right leg, getting full extension at the hip, knee, and ankle.
3. Balance on your left leg at the top of the movement.
4. Repeat for the required number of repetitions on one side and then the other.

## Coaching Tips

- Keep your chest up.
- Focus on flexing at the hip, knees, and ankles.
- Maintain a neutral back position and level hips throughout.

# Half-Kneeling Bungee Pec Fly

## Purpose

This is an upper-body strengthening exercise requiring core and hip stabilization.

## Setup

Kneel down on your right knee with your left foot forward and resting flat on the floor. A resistance band or cable column is anchored on your right-hand side. There should be some tension in either the resistance band or cable in this starting position.

## Instructions

1. Maintain a tall torso, keeping your hips tall and forward, and brace with your abdominals to help support your torso.

2. With a soft bend in your right elbow, use the muscles in your chest and shoulders to bring your hand from out to your side to straight in front of your chest.

3. Hold this position momentarily. Feel the contraction in your chest and the front of your shoulder.

4. Return to the starting position.

5. Complete all repetitions on one side and then perform on the other side.

## Coaching Tip

- Resist the temptation to lean away from the bungee or resistance.

# Push-Up and Reach

## Purpose

This is an upper-body strengthening exercise requiring core stabilization.

## Setup

Begin in the top position of a push-up.

## Instructions

1. As you lower yourself into the push-up position, slide one arm along the floor as far as you comfortably can while still maintaining a neutral back position.

2. You will feel this working your upper body, shoulder, and torso. You should not feel it in your back. If you feel your back straining, you are reaching too far.

3. Focus on stabilizing your torso as you push and pull your way back up to the starting position of your push-up.

## Coaching Tips

- Do this exercise on a smooth floor. You may place your hand on a towel to make it slide easier.

- If you have shoulder dysfunction or pain, eliminate this exercise from your routine.

# Reverse Crease Bungee Push

## Purpose

This is a goalie-specific drill to strengthen the hip, adductors, and external rotators.

## Setup

Kneel on your left knee with a medium-resistance bungee attached to your right ankle and your right leg extended straight out to the side (see photo *a*).

## Instructions

1. Maintain level shoulders and a stable torso as you recover your foot up underneath your hip (see photo *b*).
2. Extend your leg back out to the starting position (see photo *a*).
3. Perform the required number of reps before switching legs and repeating on the other side.

## Coaching Tips

- Make sure you stay tall in your torso throughout the exercise.
- If you have access to a smooth surface, removing your shoes and letting your socks slide on the floor will improve the quality of the exercise.

# Squat Jump and Hold

## Purpose

This is a leg power and stamina exercise that teaches you to be explosive when fatigued.

## Setup

Stand with feet hip-width apart.

## Instructions

1. Perform three squat jumps using proper mechanics and jumping as high as you can, as quickly as you can.

2. Upon completion of the three jumps, immediately lower into a squat position with your thighs parallel to the floor and your chest in a neutral position (do not round your back). Hold this position for five seconds.

3. Upon completion of the five-second hold, immediately return to three squat jumps, jumping as high and as quickly as you can.

4. Repeat this cycle of three jumps and a five-second hold six times.

## Coaching Tips

- Maintain perfect posture during the squat and hold. Do not rest your arms on your legs. Do not round your back.
- The ideal squat position is with your thighs parallel to the floor.

# Contra Dumbbell Row

## Purpose

This is an upper-body strengthening exercise and hip stabilization drill.

## Setup

Stand on your left foot with your torso and right leg parallel to the floor. Hold a dumbbell in your right hand.

## Instructions

1. Using your right arm, row the weight up until it touches the lower portion of your ribcage.
2. Squeeze your shoulder blade back slightly as you row.
3. Return to the starting position.

## Coaching Tips

- You will feel fatigue on the outside of your stabilizing hip as you go through this exercise.
- Make sure to maintain a straight back position.

# Three-Way Medicine Ball Squeeze

## Purpose

This is a strengthening exercise for your groin muscles.

## Setup

Lie on the floor, holding a medicine ball between your knees.

## Instructions

1. Begin with your feet off the floor and your knees pulled up higher than your navel.
2. Maintain a neutral back position with your back resting on the floor.
3. Push into the ball, gradually generating maximum tension for 15 seconds. Now, lower your legs slightly so your knees are right above your hips.
4. Again, squeeze the medicine ball, gradually building tension over 15 seconds.
5. Put your feet back flat on the floor with your knees bent 90 degrees, and squeeze the medicine ball for 15 more seconds.

## Coaching Tip

- Gradually increase the tension you put on the medicine ball, using your adductors (groin muscles) to squeeze increasingly harder.

# SPEED, POWER, AND AGILITY TRAINING

Picture a sliding post-to-post desperation save. It is clear that the goaltender relied on his speed, power, and agility and maybe luck to get there. What you may not realize is how speed, power, and agility also let goaltenders play with more patience. Goaltenders with speed and power don't have to make their move as quickly; they can wait an extra split second to get a better read on the shot.

Goaltenders with more speed, power, and agility also use less energy than less powerful or efficient goaltenders. The improved efficiency lets them keep more gas in the tank throughout the game so they have it when they really need it, such as when their team gets a penalty in overtime.

There are many ways to develop power, which is measured by how quickly goaltenders can produce force. The quicker goaltenders can produce force, the more powerful they are and the faster they will be. Agility is the ability of a goaltender to start, stop, and change direction quickly; it requires speed, but also skill. Your goal is to complete these movements with speed, skill, and balance so you are prepared to move in any direction at any time.

A common error is trying to focus on power training before developing the base of mobility, strength, and skill in the movement patterns that are often used for power training, such as jumping, hopping, and bounding. By following the progressions in this book, you are setting yourself up for success.

## The Difference Between Quick Feet and Agility

Having "quick feet" is different from being agile. Have you ever seen pro hockey players doing agility drills? They are low in their legs, moving quickly, but keeping their upper bodies controlled. They look athletic. Now, picture other athletes moving through the same drill. Their feet are moving quickly, but their arms are flailing around, and their torsos are leaning from side to side; they just don't look athletic. Both sets of athletes could be said to have quick feet, but only the NHL players in this example are demonstrating great agility.

What you want when you train for agility is to be using the right amount of force, in the right direction, with precision and efficiency. This means staying low in the legs, flexing at the ankles so you're not on your tiptoes, and executing the pattern properly.

## Speed, Power, and Agility Training Programs

Here are two tables outlining two sample speed, power, and agility programs for you to include in your training (see tables 7.7 and 7.8). Remember to complete a dynamic warm-up before starting these workouts. Also, try to do these workouts when you are fresh so you can get maximum power. If you are already fatigued heading into your speed, power, and agility workout, you will not get the maximum benefit. Remember that your speed, power, and agility should be hard from a focus and concentration perspective because you're trying to move your body faster than you ever have before, utilizing both efficiency and precision. However, the sessions should not be overly fatiguing from an output perspective. If you're feeling exhausted during your speed session, you are not training speed; you are actually training stamina, which we cover in the next section. In these workouts, you can rest between exercises. Notice that I have included some mobility drills, such as the quadruped hip circles, pigeon flow, and butterfly flow, to give you a natural rest break, but if you are starting to fatigue and feel sluggish, take an extra rest break.

## Speed, Power, and Agility Exercises

This section includes the exercises listed in the speed, power, and agility training programs (tables 7.7 and 7.8). Take time to learn how to do the movements with perfect technique before you add speed. Stay low in your legs and maintain level hips and shoulders.

## Table 7.7   Speed, Power, and Agility Training Program 1

| Exercise | Sets* | Reps | Tempo | Page numbers |
|---|---|---|---|---|
| Lateral hop and stick | 2 | 3 each direction | Hold 2 sec | 182 |
| Quadruped hip circles | 2 | 5 each direction | Slow | 183 |
| V drill | 2 | 4 each direction | Fast | 184 |
| Knee recovery lateral hop and shuffle | 2 | 3 each direction | Fast | 185 |
| Wide out | 2 | 8 reps | Fast | 186 |

*Complete two sets of the exercises with two minutes of rest between circuits (you can work on stickhandling or eye-hand coordination during this rest).

## Table 7.8   Speed, Power, and Agility Training Program 2

| Exercise | Sets | Reps | Tempo | Page numbers |
|---|---|---|---|---|
| Kneeling shimmy | 3 | 3 each direction | Easy | 187 |
| Pigeon flow | 3 | 2 each direction | Slow | 188 |
| Quick step and lateral hop | 3 | 3 each direction | Fast | 189 |
| Butterfly flow | 3 | 2 each direction | Slow | 156 |
| Quick lateral shuffle to knee down | 3 | 3 each direction | Fast | 190 |

*Complete two sets of the exercises with two minutes of rest between circuits (you can work on stickhandling or eye-hand coordination during this rest).

# Lateral Hop and Stick

## Purpose

This is a power and agility exercise requiring deceleration and balance.

## Setup

Stand on the floor with good footing so you will not slip. Stand on your right foot with your hip, knee, and ankle bent. This should almost mirror your ready position.

## Instructions

1. Quickly hop laterally from your right to your left foot.
2. Hop back to your right foot, and hold that position with perfect balance for a minimum of two seconds.
3. Repeat for the required number of repetitions, and then switch starting leg.

## Coaching Tips

- The goal is to establish perfect deceleration and balance, so take your time getting your balance before you start increasing the distance that you hop.
- When you land with perfect balance, your hips and shoulders will be level, and your body will be in a perfect neutral position, similar to your ready stance.

# Quadruped Hip Circles

## Purpose

This is a rotator cuff exercise for your hips, requiring core stabilization.

## Setup

Kneel on all fours. Bring your right heel as close to your right buttock as possible.

## Instructions

1. Keeping the heel as close to your buttock as possible, trace as a big a circle as you can with your knee (the movement will be coming from your hip) without twisting your pelvis or moving your torso.

2. Go slowly and imagine you're stirring a pot of honey with your knee, generating internal resistance in the hip rotators.

3. Repeat the required number of repetitions both clockwise and counterclockwise.

## Coaching Tip

- Make sure there is no movement in your pelvis or torso.

# V Drill

## Purpose

This is an agility drill that helps you move forward and backward on a diagonal.

## Setup

Imagine that you are standing at your right post in your ready position.

## Instructions

1. Start in a low ready position.
2. Push forward and laterally off your right leg as though moving from your right post to the top center of your crease. Establish your ready position as if you were preparing for a shot.
3. Then, pivot as you would on the ice, push off your right leg, again moving down and back as though moving to your left post. Establish your ready position as if preparing for a shot.
4. Repeat in the other direction for the required number of repetitions.

## Coaching Tip

- Visualize a play developing as you go through this drill. Ask yourself where you should be looking and where your glove and blocker should be.

# Knee Recovery Lateral Hop and Shuffle

## Purpose

This agility drill requires vertical and horizontal agility.

## Setup

Get into a tall kneeling position on the floor.

## Instructions

1. From the tall kneeling position, recover your right foot underneath your hip, placing it flat on the floor, and immediately drive into a full lateral push, hopping to your left. You will start on your knees but land on your left foot.

2. As soon as you land on your left foot, take two quick shuffles back to your starting position, staying on your feet.

3. Take your time to return to the tall kneeling position for your next rep. Do not slam down onto your knees as though you are on the ice with your gear on.

## Coaching Tips

- Keep your shoulders and pelvis level as you drive laterally. Do not let your torso bend to the side.
- Think of where your glove hand and stick should be positioned. Mimic those postures.

# Wide Out

## Purpose

This agility drill helps you close your five-hole and strengthen your groin muscles dynamically.

## Setup

Stand on the floor in a squat position with a neutral back.

## Instructions

1. Maintain your low position. Your head should not bounce up and down.
2. Quickly hop your feet out to a double hip-width stance, toes pointing slightly out, knees staying over the toes.
3. Immediately hop back to your starting position with your feet together, making sure you close both your feet and your knees in.

## Coaching Tip

- Concentrate on making these quick, explosive movements.

# Kneeling Shimmy

## Purpose

This agility drill is done in a knee-down position.

## Setup

Kneel on the floor, wearing knee pads.

## Instructions

1. Stay tall in your hips. Do not sit back on your buttocks.
2. Quickly step or shimmy three steps to your right.
3. Immediately shimmy back to your left in an equal number of steps.

## Coaching Tips

- Start slowly and gradually build speed. The movement will take some getting used to.
- Maintain level shoulders and hips. Take quick, small steps rather than big extended pushes.
- You must wear knee pads for this drill.

# Pigeon Flow

## Purpose

This dynamic mobility drill helps you develop stability and control through the hip and torso.

## Setup

Assume a static pigeon stretch position on the floor with the right leg tucked under the body and the left leg extended behind.

## Instructions

1. Attempt to lift the left leg straight off the floor as you use your right hip to come into a single-leg tall kneeling position.
2. Once your left leg is off the floor and your hips are raised into a single-leg kneeling position, sweep the left leg around in front of your body without touching the foot to the floor.
3. Slowly return to your starting position without touching the floor or using your hands.

## Coaching Tips

- Go slowly. The slower you go, the harder it will be.
- Try not to use your hands at all.
- Focus on slightly bracing with your abdominals to help improve your core stability.

# Quick Step and Lateral Hop

## Purpose

This agility drill helps you with lateral movement using quick, small pushes and big post-to-post pushes.

## Setup

Stand in a low athletic position with your head and chest up and hips, knees, and ankles flexed. Your feet should be hip width or slightly wider.

## Instructions

1. Push off your left foot with two quick steps to your right, stay low, and don't let your torso sway.
2. At the end of your second push, you will land on your right foot and decelerate the landing by flexing at your hip, knee, and ankle.
3. Decelerate and then immediately explode off the right leg to get all the way back to your starting point in one big push.
4. Land back in your low ready position and repeat. Perform all repetitions on one side and then repeat in the other direction.

## Coaching Tips

- Stay low in your legs.
- Think of where your glove and blocker should be.
- Think of where you should be looking so your head leads the movement.

# Quick Lateral Shuffle to Knee Down

## Purpose

This agility drill requires both horizontal and vertical agility.

## Setup

Stand on the floor in your ready position with knee pads on.

## Instructions

1. Perform two quick lateral pushes to your left.
2. Upon completion of the two quick pushes, drop your right knee to the floor, lightly touching it.
3. Immediately push off your left leg and perform two quick shuffles back to your right.
4. Immediately drop your left knee to the floor.

## Coaching Tips

- Stay tall in your torso and hips throughout this drill.
- As you shuffle laterally, keep your shoulders and hips level. Do not bend to the side.

# STAMINA TRAINING

Since the goaltending position requires quick, explosive movements, it is more beneficial to go hard for a shorter duration and then recover. Your "shifts" are unpredictable. You need to move and train in all directions, including vertical movements. Those are exhausting. Think of your team down two players on a penalty kill where you are moving from your post lean, down to your butterfly, recovering again, and moving post to post.

There is an incredible amount of stamina required for those movements. But this is not the type of stamina you develop when you do long, steady cardio, which you do not need to do. Rather, you need to train the way you will play. You need to be focused on executing your stamina drills with precision. Keep your movements crisp even when you are tired. Bad training habits will translate onto the ice. Do you ever drop your gloves as you get tired? Do you stand up in your legs when you fatigue? You must practice staying low, maintaining your glove and blocker position, and executing with precision and purpose. When you build your stamina like this, you'll be able to keep your focus and speed even into overtime. It will also give you another key ingredient for success—confidence.

Your stamina training will never get easier, unfortunately. If you find yourself completing one of these stamina workouts and thinking to yourself, "I'm getting so fit that this is easy for me; I'm in great shape," it means you did not push yourself enough. Even the fittest human being will be exhausted doing 30- to 60-second interval repeats. It does not get easier; you just cover more ground and you work more explosively.

## Stamina Training Programs

Here are three sample stamina training programs that you can use for your off-ice training (see tables 7.9–7.11). Do your stamina training after your strength training or on a separate day. You do not want to burn up all the gas in your tank before hitting the gym for your strength session, which is a priority. Don't worry if your legs are a bit heavy going into your stamina session; it's going to be tough anyway. And remember, you should complete a dynamic warm-up before starting these workouts.

## Stamina Exercises

This section includes the exercises listed in the stamina training programs (tables 7.9–7.11). As you fatigue, you will naturally slip back into your old habits. Focus on maintaining your good form throughout the workouts, bend your knees, get up to speed quickly, and move with efficiency.

## Table 7.9 Stamina Training Program 1

| Exercise* | Sets | Reps/duration** |
|---|---|---|
| 20 sec full out, then 10 sec very, very easy | Perform one set of each exercise. | 8 times |
| Very, very easy | | 3 minutes |
| 20 sec full out, then 10 sec very, very easy | | 6 times |
| Very, very easy | | 2 minutes |
| 20 sec full out, then 10 sec very, very easy | | 4 times |

*Types of exercises: running, agility drills, skipping rope, stationary bike, and slide board.

**Do not rest between exercises.

## Table 7.10 Stamina Training Program 2

| Exercise* | Sets | Reps/duration** | Page numbers |
|---|---|---|---|
| High-knees jump rope | 6 | 30 sec | 193 |
| Alternate-knee recovery | | 4 each leg leading | 194 |
| Squat jump and hold | | 3 jumps with 10-sec hold × 4 | 176 |
| Quick step and lateral hop | | 4 each direction | 189 |
| Side plank and rotate | | 2 × 30 sec on each side | 195 |

*Types of exercises: running, agility drills, skipping rope, stationary bike, and slide board.

**Rest two minutes after each set of exercises. Do not rest between individual exercises.

## Table 7.11 Stamina Training Program 3

| Exercise | | Reps/duration | Sets | Page numbers |
|---|---|---|---|---|
| Superset A | A1. 200-yd shuttle run | 2 | 4 sets with 2 minutes of rest between | 196 |
| | A2. Quick step and lateral hop | 4 each direction | | 189 |
| Superset B | B1. 200-yd shuttle run | 2 | 3 sets with 2 minutes of rest between | 196 |
| | B2. Alternate-knee recovery | 4 each side | | 194 |
| 100-yd shuttle run | | 4 | 1 set only. Rest for 60 sec between each repetition. | 196 |

# High-Knees Jump Rope

## Purpose

This is an energy system drill using the hip flexors.

## Setup

Find an open area where you can skip rope.

## Instructions

Perform quick skipping in a running fashion, bringing the knees up high with each step. The goal is to get your knee as high as your navel without rounding your lower back while staying quick and light on your feet.

## Coaching Tip

- If you struggle with skipping, start this exercise with regular two-foot skipping until your skill level improves.

# Alternate-Knee Recovery

## Purpose

This agility drill helps you recover one skate underneath your hips from a butterfly position.

## Setup

Kneel on the floor with your hips forward and your torso tall.

## Instructions

1. Without standing all the way up in the legs, recover one foot underneath your hips, followed by your other foot, and then return to the starting position. In other words, bring your right foot up underneath you, then your left foot up underneath you, and then return to your right knee and your left knee.

2. Repeat the required number of repetitions leading with your right foot and the required number of repetitions leading with your left foot.

## Coaching Tips

- Your head should stay almost in the same position throughout the drill. It should not be bobbing up and down.

- You may wish to wear your knee pads for this drill, but do not slam your knees down as though you are in a game on the ice with all your gear on. Keep it quick and light.

# Side Plank and Rotate

## Purpose

This is a core stabilization exercise that challenges you to maintain a stable torso through different planes of motion.

## Setup

Take a side plank position with your right elbow on the floor.

## Instructions

1. With your right elbow on the floor, position your left foot forward and your right foot backward. They will not be stacked on top of each other.
2. Hold this side plank position for the required duration.
3. At the end of the required duration, roll your hips and shoulders simultaneously to a front plank position. Lift your right shoulder and hip up to finish in a left side plank position.

## Coaching Tip

- There should be no twisting in your torso as you rotate from one side to the other. It will require a lot of core strength to keep everything in a straight line.

# Shuttle Run

## Purpose

This is a pure stamina drill that will work on change of direction under fatigue and build mental toughness.

## Setup

Measure out either 100 or 200 yards in 25-yard increments on a level surface with good footing where you can run safely.

## Instructions

1. Sprint from the starting cone to the 25-yard cone and back two times for 100 yards or four times for 200 yards.
2. Use both legs to help decelerate and change direction. Get back up to speed as quickly as possible after changing direction.

## Coaching Tip

- Perform this drill on the grass wearing soccer or football cleats for good footing.

# CREATING WEEKLY TRAINING SCHEDULES

The off-season is a key time for you to build your mobility, stability, strength, speed, and stamina, but you need to continue training during your season so you continue to improve throughout the year. Your training schedules and priorities will differ during the season and in the off-season.

## In-Season Training Schedules

During the season, the focus is on speed, power, and staying healthy. Focus on your explosive power and your max strength, and keep the injury bug at bay by working on mobility and getting adequate recovery. If you are not playing regularly, then you also need to make up for the lack of stamina training you would get from games. I know it seems unfair because you are at the games and putting in the time, but your body doesn't know that. You will lose stamina if you do not put in the extra effort to make up for it away from the rink. Don't be one of the goaltenders who ignores in-season training and ends up slower, weaker, and more vulnerable to injury when playoffs roll around. You also don't want to try to maintain your off-season training schedule during the season, with the added volume of your practices and games.

Table 7.12 provides a sample in-season training schedule, showing two team practices and two games.

## Off-Season Training Schedules

During the off-season, you will follow a periodized training program, which is beyond the scope of this book, but essentially you will progress through different training phases—begin with a foundation, build functional strength, build max strength, and then build power. There are many different schemes you can use, but that's the general idea. It's the same way you would build a house—dig out the basement, put up the studs, add the drywall, and install the home theater.

Tables 7.13 and 7.14 show two different off-season training schedules. One uses a full-body routine that you will complete three days per week. The other uses an upper- and lower-body split. Notice how stamina and strength are on the same day in the three-days-per-week program and on the lower-body day in the split program. Speed is either by itself or paired with your upper-body workout.

This schedule doesn't mean you have to do your strength workouts on Monday, Wednesday, and Friday if you're doing a full-body routine. You should

Table 7.12 **Sample In-Season Training Schedule**

| Monday | Tuesday | Wednesday | Thursday | Friday | Saturday | Sunday |
|---|---|---|---|---|---|---|
| Practice | Strength and speed | Practice | Strength and speed | Game | Game | |
| Mobility | Mobility | Mobility | Mobility | Mobility | Mobility | |
| Optional: stamina | | Optional: stamina | | | | |

Table 7.13 **Sample Off-Season Training Schedule: Full Body**

| Monday | Tuesday | Wednesday | Thursday | Friday | Saturday | Sunday |
|---|---|---|---|---|---|---|
| Strength | | Strength | | Strength | | |
| Stamina | Speed | Stamina | Speed | | Stamina | |
| Mobility | Mobility | Mobility | Mobility | Mobility | Mobility | |

Table 7.14 **Sample Off-Season Training Schedule: Upper-and-Lower Body**

| Monday | Tuesday | Wednesday | Thursday | Friday | Saturday | Sunday |
|---|---|---|---|---|---|---|
| Lower-body strength | Upper-body strength | Recovery or prehab | Lower-body strength | Upper-body strength | | |
| Stamina | Speed | | Stamina | Speed | Stamina | |
| Mobility | Mobility | Mobility | Mobility | Mobility | Mobility | |

fit your schedule. For you, your workouts might be on Tuesday, Thursday, and Saturday or Tuesday, Thursday, and Sunday. What you should avoid is working the same muscle groups two days in a row.

During your mobility, strength, speed, and stamina training, make a mental connection between your training and on-ice performance. Acknowledge what you are trying to train and how each exercise will help you on the ice. Use perfect form and be consistent. Those are the two key ingredients for success.

# Chapter 8

# The Mental Game

Pete Fry

In chapter 7, we discussed the importance of off-ice training. We focused on mobility, strength, speed, agility, and stamina training for goaltenders. These physical components are extremely important for you to train and continuously improve on throughout your goaltending career. But what about the mental side of your game? It has been said that goaltending is 90 percent mental. If so, then why isn't 90 percent of training devoted to the mental part of the game? In fact, why is so little time devoted to the mental portion of the goaltender's repertoire? Skill development in goaltending has come a long way over the past few decades. Years ago, skill development for goaltenders was very limited. Now, the mental development of goaltenders is in about the same place the skill development was in the 1980s.

Here, we give the mental side of the game the necessary focus it deserves to help you be successful as a goaltender. In this chapter, we discuss the importance of a complete goaltender mindset. We look at the three major components that make up this mindset: focus, confidence, and visualization. We tie them all together with an explanation of mind mapping and how it can benefit your mental preparation. Also, we include exercises for you to perform aimed at improving your goaltending mindset. If you learn or do something once, it creates a temporary neural pathway in the brain that, if not reinforced, goes away. On the contrary, if you keep repeating an action or mental exercise, it strengthens the pathway. So remember, it is as important if not more to exercise your brain as your body.

# THE IMPORTANCE OF MINDSET

Working on your mindset may be the most impactful thing you practice as a goalie. What makes the difference between a great and an average goalie? Mindset. Think of a game in which you played spectacularly. Now, think of a game in which you struggled. What was the difference? Was your equipment significantly different? Probably not. Was your physical conditioning significantly different? Probably not. Were your goalie skills significantly different? Probably not. Was your mindset significantly different? Most likely, yes. You must work on the goalie mindset consistently, and it will improve much like your biceps will get bigger if you do bicep curls consistently. This is not to discount the importance of your equipment, physical skills, or goaltending skills. However, the fastest way to elevate your game is to work on your mindset, specifically the three areas we discuss and develop in this chapter.

Montreal Canadiens goaltending great Ken Dryden expressed the mindset aspect of goaltending:

> *Because the demands on a goalie are mostly mental, it means that for a goalie, the biggest enemy is himself. Not a puck, not an opponent, not a quirk of size or style. Him. The stress and anxiety he feels when he plays . . . [is] in constant ebb and flow, but never disappearing. The successful goalie understands these neuroses, accepts them, and puts them under control. The unsuccessful goalie is distracted by them, his mind in knots, his body quickly following.*

What Ken Dryden said was that all goaltenders can have negative thoughts, but the goaltenders who can control those negative thoughts will be successful, whereas the others will think themselves out of stopping the puck.

Hall of Fame goaltender Patrick Roy of the Montreal Canadiens and Colorado Avalanche talked about the power of his mind helping him to achieve more than almost any other goaltender in the game. Read part of Roy's Hockey Hall of Fame induction speech translated from French:

> *My journey through the NHL, with Montreal, and then Colorado, is loaded with special memories and emotions. My first memory goes back to when I was about 8 years old when my parents brought me to the arena for the first time. It was then that I started believing in my dream: becoming a professional goaltender in the National Hockey League. It was at that moment that I chose to dedicate myself entirely to it, gaining inspiration from the likes of Daniel Bouchard and Rogie Vachon, while [sic] every ounce of my heart, my guts, and my passion. I dreamt of this league where*

*only the best played! I dreamt of being one of its stars and being a winner! I dreamt of playing alongside the game's greats! I dreamt that my talent, my inner strength, and my never-ending desire to win, would rock hockey fans!*

www.habseyesontheprize.com/2008/09/patrick-roy-hhof-induction-speech.html

You will notice at the outset that Patrick Roy had a clear picture in his mind of being one of the greatest goalies ever to have played the game. He had the success mindset whereby he envisioned greatness and then set out to achieve it.

# MINDSET TECHNIQUES

There are three mindset techniques that you must work on to be successful as a goaltender: focus, confidence, and visualization.

## Total Focus for Goaltenders

Focusing on something is not simply the act of passively looking at it. Focusing requires you to direct your attention to it completely, see it in detail, crisply and clearly identifying every aspect of it. Hold a magnifying glass over a piece of paper with a beam of sunlight directed through it. If you hold the magnifying glass still for long enough, the paper will start on fire. If you move your hand slightly, the focus of the sunbeam through the glass will shift and no fire will be started. Picture the sunlight being your brain and the magnifying glass, your personal focus and attention. If you hold your focus long enough, you will "be on fire." When you hear someone say, "that goaltender is on fire," this is exactly what is happening. If you are unfocused, you are probably not stopping many pucks. Therefore, focus is one of the three most important mental areas to practice.

You need this magnifying glass–like focus in five key areas: breathing, players, stance, moment, and puck. To help you remember these key areas, associate each with a well-known professional goaltender.

### Brodeur = Breathing

Focus your attention on your breathing. Take two or three slow, deep breaths in through your nose and out through your mouth. Maintain a ratio of one to two, with a one-second inhale to a two-second exhale. For example, if you breathe in for three seconds, then exhale for six seconds. With each inhalation, feel the air coming in through your nose and filling your lungs. As you exhale, imagine anxiety or stress leaving your body with your air. Feel the air leaving your lungs and coming out of your mouth. Can you feel your breath going in and out? Is it steady? Is it natural? Is it deep or shallow? Are you holding your breath unconsciously? Now, change your breathing from deep to regular breaths. Notice that your nerves are calm and your mind, clear and attentive. By focusing on your breathing, you bring your mind home to your body. You create space and release stress. This allows you to focus.

### Price = Players

Focus on the players on the other team. Notice how each player is positioned and which way he shoots. What threats are there? What direction are the players skating? With this knowledge, you will be able to predict what plays are developing, how far you need to move across your crease on backdoor plays, and more. This is how you develop "goalie sense," which allows you to anticipate where the play is headed; this is comparable to "hockey sense" for players and is a form of soft focus (refer to chapter 2 for a discussion on hard and soft focus).

### Schneider = Stance

No matter what sport you play, stance is always one of the key components. As a goaltender, everything starts from a balanced stance. Are your feet properly positioned? Is your body correctly positioned and weighted properly on your two feet? Are your hands in the right position? Do you feel totally balanced in your stance? For more information about stance, refer to chapter 2.

### Markstrom = Moment

Being in the moment is critical. What is happening right now is the most important moment in your life. The only time you can do something about anything is right now. In previous chapters, you learned about hard and soft focus and how to direct your attention. You learned how to read and respond to plays. You focused on your opponents to identify where they are on the ice and how they shoot. You practiced all your stance and movement techniques. Now, in this moment, you must allow your training to come through as you respond to what is taking place around you. It's not about what happened last game or last period or even last minute. What is happening right now? Focus only on the present. Be in the moment.

### Pavelec = Puck

As a goaltender, your job is to stop the puck. To stop it, you must see it, which requires your focus on the puck 100 percent of the time. Are you focused on the puck? To help you, try focusing on the dots or the words on the puck or the center of the puck.

For easy reference, you can now associate each element with an NHL goaltender: breathing with Brodeur, players with Price, stance with Schneider, moment with Markstrom, and puck with Pavelec. Now that you know what the components of focus are, when and how do you use it in a game? Goaltenders must adjust their focus level as the play moves from the opposite end of the ice all the way to their net.

1. When the play is at the other end or if you are waiting for a face-off anywhere on the ice, focus on your breathing. Feel your breathing; hear your breathing. This will relax and calm you, clear your mind, and allow you to prepare for what's next.

2. After steadying your breathing, when the play is at the other end or when you are waiting for a face-off, focus on where the players on the other team are. Which way do they shoot? What patterns are forming as they break up ice toward you?

3. Next, when the play gets to center, start to focus on your stance. Be totally balanced in your stance and in the right position in your crease.

4. As the play gets to the blue line, focus 100 percent on being in the moment. What's happening right now?

5. Once you are in the moment, then focus 100 percent on the puck. See it leave the stick blade and see it hit your body.

Upon mastering your focus skills, your game, goals against average, save percentage, win-loss record, and the number of shutouts you have will improve. Remember, there's focus and then there's "laser-like focus." The more you practice, the better you will get. And we have great focus exercises for you at the end of this chapter.

# Total Confidence for Goaltenders

There is one skill that can carry you through and impact a game, a season, and a career. That one skill is confidence. How do you obtain it so it will be impactful on your game, season, career, and life? A goaltender must be the most confident player on the ice. But what is confidence? You don't learn what confidence is in school. When asking goalies what confidence is, few can provide the correct answer. This section clarifies what confidence is. From here, you can work on improving and mastering your confidence.

The definition of confidence is the belief or conviction that an outcome will be favorable, the belief that you will win. If you are a student, confidence is the belief that you will pass the test before you take it. If you are a golfer, confidence is the conviction that you will put the ball on the green before you even swing at the ball. If you are going for a job interview, confidence is the feeling that you will get the job before the interview even starts. If you are an entrepreneur, confidence is the certainty that your company will be successful even though it is just in the idea stage. Or if you are a public speaker, confidence is the trust in yourself that you will hold the audience spellbound and deliver the greatest speech before you even get in front of the crowd.

Confidence is knowing and having the feeling that you will be successful even before you begin. In goaltending terms, it means having the feeling of knowing you are going to make the save before the puck leaves the player's stick. It is the feeling of knowing you are going to win the game before the puck has dropped or that you are going to win the championship before you even play your first game of the season. Once you know exactly what confidence is, you will have clarity, and confidence will be a lot easier to obtain.

Now that you know what confidence is, where does it come from and how do you obtain it? Confidence in goaltending is derived from two things: what you focus on and how you move. To help you remember this, think of FM: focus and movement.

Some people may argue that confidence comes from experience and doing well at something. But the only reason you may be more confident once you have done well at something is because you have experience with it. Experience is more about competence than confidence. Being competent at something does not guarantee you will be confident. Think of Tiger Woods, for example. Some would say he is the greatest golfer of all time; yet even though he has lots of experience and has hit the ball successfully many times, they do not guarantee he is confident. He has had many failures lately because of lack of confidence. If someone with lots of experience is confident, it is because they are focused on what they have done well.

Let's break down these two components for you so you completely understand. When you gain full comprehension of something, it is easier for you to achieve.

## What You Focus On

Let's talk about the first half of obtaining confidence—what to focus on. To be specific, this is the outcome you focus on, how you focus on it, and the words you say as well as the questions you ask yourself.

To be confident, focus on the outcome you want. Set your goals for the long term (i.e., career), the season, and the game. Be specific and clear on the results you want to achieve, what you need to work on to make the desired outcome a reality, and what your expectations are. Write them down, visualize them, and repeat them to yourself frequently to ensure that you remain focused on your goals. Be really clear on the outcome you want. Be clear on your expectations. For example, if you were to ask most goalies, "When do you feel the most confident?" they would often respond the same: "After I make a couple of big saves." However, they don't need to make those big saves to feel confident. They simply need to picture in their minds the saves being made even before the game starts.

Several years ago, there was a goaltender named Lance Mayes who was playing in the British Columbia Hockey League. Before every game started, he would visualize sitting in the dressing room at the end of the game looking at the game puck. You know why he would do that and what that would mean? That puck represented Lance's getting a shutout. This image and focus would bring the feelings of confidence to Lance during the visualization process. Additionally, Lance would be able to bring those feelings back during the game to feel confident before he even made his first save.

On the other end of the spectrum, there was another goaltender who made a huge jump in his career. Jordan Watt had never played on a rep team; he jumped from playing house hockey to the Western Hockey League. One time during the summer, Jordan was having a rough training session. When asked what he was focusing on during the session, Jordan said he was focusing on letting pucks in. He kept picturing letting pucks in, in his mind. This created an unconfident state with poor expectations. This was a great learning lesson for Jordan. He learned to reshape his focus to see himself making saves instead of letting goals in. Jordan now uses these focusing techniques in his current law practice.

## How You Move

Let's now talk about the second aspect of confidence: how you move, or what is also referred to as your body language. When you are playing well, how do you move? When you are confident, are your shoulders slouched forward or pulled back? They are back. Is your chin pointed downward or is it raised? It is raised. Is your head looking down or up? It is up. Is your breathing quick and shallow or slow and deep? It is slow and deep. Are your facial muscles downward or upward? They are tight and upward.

As an exercise, stand up and walk around the room like you are confident. Lift your chin, put your shoulders back, and raise your facial muscles. Raise your chest and breathe deep, slow breaths deeply into your abdomen and slowly back out. You will find that by doing this, by moving in a confident manner, you are starting to feel confident. Now, try this. Instead of looking up, look down at the ground. Slouch your shoulders forward. Relax your facial muscles. Point your chin to the ground. Breathe quickly and shallowly. Picture how a person who is depressed stands and stand like that. How are you feeling now? Not so confident, right?

When you see the word confident, snap yourself back into a confident physical state. Ready . . . "confident." Head up, chin up, shoulders back, breath deep and slow, facial muscles raised and tighter. Feeling confident? Now, when you see the word depressed, go back to how a depressed person would stand. Ready . . . "depressed." Look down at the ground. Slouch your shoulders forward. Relax your facial muscles. Point your chin to the ground. Breathe quickly and shallowly. Picture how a person who is depressed stands and stand like that. How are you feeling now? Not so confident again, right? Now, when you see the word confident, whip yourself back into a confident state. Ready . . . "confident." Quickly put your head up, chin up, and shoulders back, and breathe deeply and slowly and raise and tighten your facial muscles. Feeling confident?

Get good at doing this. Become great at being able to whip yourself into a state of confidence from a state of not so confident. You should now understand the power of movement for confidence.

# Total Visualization for Goaltenders

Visualization is a form of self-creating memories and therefore prepares you for how to react to a given situation. This is why visualization is one of the top three mental skills to work on. Visualization can be defined as the formation of mental visual images.

## The Conscious and Subconscious Mind

Everyone has a conscious and a subconscious mind. The conscious mind controls our thinking and actions while we are awake. For example, running, jumping, speaking, and performing tasks are controlled by our conscious mind. The subconscious mind reacts instantly, drawing on our habits. The subconscious mind can be called "the file folder of our future." The subconscious mind does not distinguish between good and bad, true and false, what is real and what is imagined. It is like the most powerful data storage device on the planet.

When your subconscious mind is given an image or thought repeatedly, it will go to work to bring the image or thought to reality. For this reason, it is important that you fill your subconscious mind with as much positive imagery as possible. Your mind thinks in pictures. It is important to see pictures of what you hope to achieve and not of what you don't want to have happen. Drop clear, precise images in your subconscious mind of your desired result.

## The Practice of Visualization

Your brain is more powerful than any computer on the planet. Every second of your life, your brain is receiving thousands of external stimuli through your senses. Your brain must instantaneously decide what is important, what to ignore, and what requires action. To make these decisions, it relies on what it has learned from previous life experience. When you visualize, you are mentally practicing how to react in each situation. By visualizing, you are mentally living the experience that you are preparing for. Full visualization includes the sights, sounds, and reactions—the complete experience. By practicing visualization frequently, you are training your body and your brain how to react when the situation becomes a reality. The moment of reality is then reacted to like a prelived experience. For example, if you visualize making saves beforehand, it prepares your brain and body for the experience. On the contrary, if you have negative mental images, those, too, become the way you react. Not only does visualization help you in a game setting; it also will make you more confident because your brain and body will feel as if you have already had the positive experience.

You can reach your goals faster and more smoothly by visualizing outcomes that you want to happen. Done correctly, the impact that visualization can have is second to none. Goalies have gone from house hockey to the Western Hockey League by utilizing visualization, from being written off to having NHL careers through visualization.

A study was conducted on Olympic downhill skiers. The researchers hooked the skiers up to electrodes and asked them to visualize skiing. The electrodes picked up that their muscle fibers twitched in the same way they would if they actually were skiing. This illustrates the power of visualization. In some cases, as with the skiers, the body may respond in the same way through visualization as it would if you were actually performing the task. Now, apply that to making saves. See yourself making saves repeatedly. Repetitive visualization should translate to actual improvement on the ice.

Another study conducted by Dr. Biasiotto at the University of Chicago was done where he split people into three groups and tested each group on how many free throws they could make. After this, he had the first group practice free throws every day for an hour. The second group just visualized themselves making free throws. The third group did nothing. After 30 days, he tested them again. The first group improved by 24 percent, and the second group improved by 23 percent without even touching a basketball! The third group did not improve, which was expected.

## Visualizations for the Goaltender

You can use visualization to develop a goaltending skill more quickly. Visualize yourself being great at that skill even before you attempt it.

**Save**   You can use visualization when executing a save. Before the puck leaves the stick, see yourself making the save. Picture an opposition player skating over the blue line and winding up to take a slapshot. Imagine yourself as you determine which way the player shoots. As he winds up to take the shot, watch the puck as it leaves his stick. Imagine the puck heading to the top corner of the net on your glove side. See yourself watching the puck as it enters your glove and you close it, all the while maintaining your eyes on the glove. Then, imagine the cheers from the crowd as you just performed a highlight reel glove-hand save.

**Game**   A goaltender can use visualization for a game. Before the game starts, see yourself winning the game for your team and visualize all the saves you will make. Here's Western Hockey League goaltender Cody Porter visualizing over the phone with Pete Fry before a game:

> I want to hear the crowd cheer at the end of the game, see myself giving the stick away to a fan for getting first star. I want to also see the puck for the shutout. I see myself making a breakaway save, a two-on-one save with a pass, and a great glove save along with lots of controlled saves.

**Season**   Visualization can be used for a season. Before the season starts, visualize how you want your season to end up. Below is another visualization from Jeff Glass to Pete Fry before the start of a season:

> *I see myself taking the ice for the Toronto Maple Leafs in the final regular season game of the year. I have gone on a nine-game winning streak to finish the year, and this game makes it 10. I have made 30 saves versus the Montreal Canadiens and Carey Price through two periods. We are winning 2–0 heading into the third period. I go on to stop Alexander Radulov on a penalty shot in front of our home fans to preserve the two-goal lead.*

**Training Camps and Tryouts**   You can visualize for a tryout or training camp. Before the camp starts, see yourself on the team. The key is to always focus on your positive outcome and to keep negative images out of your thoughts.

For example, one of my past clients, Jordan Watt, didn't start playing goal until he was 14 and never played on a rep team or travel team. It was January, and Jordan was 17 at the time we started working together. I asked him, "If you could play anywhere at all next season, where would you like to play?" Jordan first answered Jr. B, then he answered Jr. A. When I then asked, "Not where you think you can play, but where you would want to play if you could?" Jordan proceeded to write down the "Western Hockey League." Before long, Jordan had himself a tryout with the Kelowna Rockets of the WHL. He was a long way off, but it was a start. Jordan would visualize playing for Kelowna daily. He wrote WHL on his bathroom mirror. We would even practice what he would say when he met the coach of the Kelowna Rockets, and midsummer Jordan drove down to Kelowna to meet him. Even though at the start of training camp Jordan was up against 17 other goalies that had either played WHL, Junior A, and Midget AAA, and Jordan had not even played on a Rep Team, never mind a AAA Team, Jordan won the spot. He was so focused, he worked like crazy to prepare, and he was in top physical condition and impressed the coaches and management enough to make the team.

**Career**   You can visualize for your career as well. An example might look like this:

> *I am playing in the National Hockey League, wearing a blue and white jersey with the white leaf logo, in front of 18,000 against the Chicago Blackhawks. With one minute left in game seven of the Stanley Cup Finals, I am making multiple saves against a six-on-five power play, and I hear the fans chant five, four, three, two, one. I look up, and we've won the game. We have won the Stanley Cup for the first time in 60 years. I hear my name called as the Conn Smythe winner, and finally I get my turn with the cup, skating around the ice with everyone cheering. I then realize what I've accomplished.*

# MIND MAPPING

A mind map is a diagram used to organize thoughts and ideas pertaining to a specific topic. The primary topic is indicated at the center of the map, with the related thoughts, concepts, resources, or ideas branching off the central point. It is a method of brainstorming and representing your ideas and thoughts in a visual, nonlinear format. This allows you to add or expand on ideas as they enter your head.

Mind maps can be used for almost any thinking or learning task, from studying a subject (e.g., learning geometry) to building better goaltending habits or planning your career. More important, the mind map can be used to set goals. The center is your primary goal, and how you plan to achieve the goal are your branches.

Here is another way to think of a mind map. Imagine you are starting your first game in the NHL, and you are playing against the New York Rangers in Madison Square Garden. You write "End of Game vs. New York Rangers in Madison Square Garden" in the middle of the circle, and then you branch off the middle circle all the outcomes you want to have happen during your first game in the NHL. For example, you can write how you want to feel after the game, what you want to see after the game, and what you want to hear after the game. This will help you become clear on your outcome and is the first step to being totally confident. That is the beauty of mind mapping. Once you begin, the possibilities are endless.

An example of how a mind map can be used to consider the elements required to achieve a long-term goal is shown in figure 8.1. Draw a circle in the center of a piece of paper, and in the center, write down your goal or objective. Draw a line out from the circle for each factor contributing to making the desired outcome a reality. As each thought is added, it can lead to subsequent thoughts that branch out to incorporate additional elements. Going through this exercise illustrates all the components that need to be considered to achieve your objective. Having a clear definition of all the steps involved in your desired achievement makes it easier to focus on and visualize your result, which in turn leads to more confidence as you progress.

Once you have set your goals and identified what you want to accomplish, you need to establish the correct mindset to make it happen. This includes visualizing the outcome as clearly and completely as you can, as outlined here:

1. See yourself already having achieved your desired outcome. If you recall from earlier in this chapter, Lance's pregame visualization of seeing himself holding the game puck at the end of the game is an example of seeing himself already having achieved what he wants to achieve.

2. When you focus on this, see it from your own eyes. This builds belief. If you are feeling unmotivated, then see it from above because this builds desire. From your own eyes, focus on seeing yourself in the dressing room after the game holding the game puck.

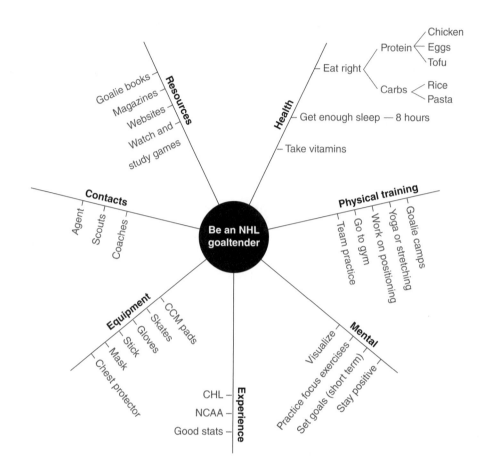

**Figure 8.1** Mind map of a career goal.

3. Add the colors into your picture. See the colors—the black puck, a blue jersey, a multicolored face mask.

4. Blow up the image in your mind really big, like you are sitting in the front row of a movie theater.

5. Move the image closer to you as if it is right in front of your face.

6. Hear the sounds you will hear. For example, will you hear your teammates cheering and celebrating? Will you hear your coach saying, "Great game!" Add the sounds.

7. Add the feelings you will feel. For example, will you feel a sense of accomplishment? Will you feel totally confident?

# GOALTENDER MINDSET DRILLS

It is just as important to go into your "Goalie Mindset Gym" daily for at least 30 minutes as it is to work on your butterfly slide or your physical conditioning. These are just a few drills you can do to strengthen your goalie mindset. Think of your goalie mindset as a muscle. It must be exercised to grow and become strong. If you neglect it, it will become weak and flabby just like any muscle you don't exercise.

## Choosing Your Words

The words you use can have a powerful effect on your desired outcome of an event. Eliminate the word don't. Your mind thinks in pictures. If I say, "Don't think of a big blue Smurf," what do you think about? Even though I said, "Don't think about it," you will think of a big blue Smurf. Your mind does not recognize the word don't. How do you utilize this? Here are some examples of what not to say and what you should replace those words with:

| Instead of saying . . . | Say this instead… |
| --- | --- |
| I will not let anything in | I will stop every puck |
| They will not score on me | I will stop them |
| I will not let in a goal | I will come up with every save |

To recap, if you are using the word don't, then you are focusing on what you don't want instead of what you do want. Remember to always think in terms of what you want. This is critical for your confidence.

Next are the questions you ask yourself. Ask yourself the right questions to be confident.

| Instead of asking . . . | Ask this instead… |
| --- | --- |
| Will they score on me? | What can I do to guarantee I make the save? |
| Will I make the save? | How can I know I will make the save? |
| Is it possible for us to beat this team? | What can I contribute to guarantee we beat this team? |

# Focus Drills

## Word Count Drill

Count the number of words on any page from this book. Focus on just this task and nothing else. If you lose count, go back to the start and begin again. When you can complete that page, then expand to two pages. To differentiate levels of focus between individuals, you can experiment by bringing several goaltenders into a room and showing a page using an overhead projector. Ask the goaltenders in the room to silently focus and count how many words are on the page. You will discover that most of the goaltenders get a different number. Sometimes one goaltender will get the correct answer. What can we conclude from this result? The result tells us that every goalie in the room has a different level of focus. If each goaltender worked on that experiment numerous times, he would start to get closer to the actual word count on the page; therefore, we could conclude that the results would be better after a certain period of focused concentration.

Now, relate this exercise to focusing on and tracking the puck. Block out all external thoughts to concentrate on the puck. Follow the puck wherever it goes on the ice. Did it flip on its side? Did it hit a player's skate? Watch as it is passed from player to player. As a shot is directed at you, continue to watch it into your body. As you practice focusing on the puck throughout all your games, it will become second nature. Since the objective of being a goaltender is to see and stop the puck, practiced focus on the puck will only improve your game.

## Focus Control Drill

Place a puck five feet away from you. Sit with your feet flat on the floor, and pick a spot on the puck where you can comfortably rest your eyes. Focus on this spot, and put the rest of your concentration on your breathing. Keeping your breath normal, concentrate on the feeling of the air coming in as you inhale and the air going out as you exhale. As you get distracted from either the puck or your breathing, catch yourself and quickly return your focus to the puck and your breath. Remember, it doesn't matter how many times you drift. It matters only that you quickly return your focus each time. Do this exercise in your room with no distractions for two minutes.

Next, place your puck on top of or beside a TV or computer. Sit far enough away from the TV that you can see the puck and the entire screen. Turn the TV on low volume, and tune it to a station you never watch. Do the same exercise, focusing on your puck and breathing, remembering to catch your focus and bring yourself back every time you get distracted by either the sound or the picture. Do this part of the exercise for one and a half minutes.

When practiced regularly for short periods, this simple exercise will help you systematically develop and strengthen your focus muscles. Soon, you will discover that you begin to catch yourself more quickly when you lose focus in your sport and can return your focus to where it belongs.

# Confidence Drills

## Positive Success Drill

For the next seven ice times, pick the three biggest successes of each ice time, and replay them in your head, big, bright, and close to you. At the same time, stand tall, shoulders back, chin up, breathing deeply. By reliving those successes and the feeling of satisfaction you gain from them, you will naturally strive to repeat that feeling.

## Self-Affirmation Drill

Write out nine positive qualities about yourself, and every morning read them aloud 10 times each in front of a mirror. When you read them, be enthusiastic, shoulders back and chin up. By reinforcing your positive attributes, you will exude more confidence on the ice.

## Save Drill

The next practice you have, put your shoulders back and your chin up while on the ice, and picture making save after save. When you picture making saves, make the images big, bright, and loud in your mind. Practice on the ice, whipping yourself into a state of confidence. For example, during a breakaway drill, picture yourself making the save even before the player touches the puck. Move in a confident way (shoulders back and chin up, with quick, intentional, and powerful movements) and make the save. Strong body language as a goaltender is the key to exuding confidence. Players need to have confidence in their goaltender. A goaltender who slouches and looks unprepared is less likely to garner the confidence of his teammates and will struggle to make saves.

# Visualization Drills

## Save Visualization and Focus Reset Drill 1

Every time you make a save, replay that save in your mind, big, bright, and close to you. See yourself making that save, repeatedly. If you don't come up with the save, smile (this reboots your brain; it's like rebooting a computer) and ask yourself, "What can I do next time to guarantee I make the save?" Then run the movie of you making the save, big, bright, and close. As in any visualization drill, seeing yourself accomplish a task before it happens increases your chances for success. When you do get scored on, it is important to reset your focus.

## Save Visualization and Focus Reset Drill 2

Watch a hockey game, preferably of your favorite team with your favorite goalie. Now, any time your favorite goalie makes a save, picture yourself as the goalie making the save. See yourself in the jersey, in full equipment, in the heat of the moment, being focused, calm, and sharp in the net. Now when you see this, make it big in your mind, see it from your own eyes, move it close, make it bright, hear the sounds, and feel the movements you are making.

This chapter focused on three key elements that will make you a stronger goaltender mentally: focus, confidence, and visualization. You learned the difference between body language that exudes confidence and that which does not. You were introduced to mind mapping, how to draw a clear picture of your goals and how you can achieve them. You learned the importance of visualization and how creating clear imagery in your mind of positive outcomes will lead to better results. Remember to practice mental training techniques just as you would any other goaltending skill that you work on daily. A strong goaltender mindset separates the elite goaltender from the average.

# Chapter 9

# Mentoring the Complete Goaltender

Goaltending is a unique position. The goaltender plays an individualized position in a team sport. Goaltenders prepare for games differently than their teammates. They have their own coaches and because they are the last line of defense, many times they find themselves the hero or the goat of individual games. It is a delicate balance for a goaltender to not get caught up in the emotional highs and lows of the position. Goalie coaches play a key role in helping the goaltender remain emotionally and physically grounded and consistent throughout a season, and they can act as a buffer between the head coach and the goaltender.

The objective of this chapter is to demonstrate Eli Wilson's philosophies and coaching methods for goaltenders. We look from the perspective of the goaltender coach, head coach, and goaltender. We analyze how the goaltender coach should prepare for practice and games, including communication with the goaltenders and the head coach. Eli believes in a positive teaching environment, and for that reason, this chapter is about the "dos" of goalie coaching, not the "don'ts." Goaltender coaches, head coaches, and goaltenders can glean information from this chapter to enhance their understanding and knowledge of the goaltending position. What can a coach do for his goaltenders both on and off the ice? What should a coach and a team expect from their goaltenders? How should the goaltender prepare himself for games and practices? How can a goaltender make himself the best teammate possible? Let's take a look!

# THE GOALIE COACH

The goaltending position continues to evolve at a rapid rate. For that reason, the need for goaltender coaches on teams at all levels has become apparent. A skilled goaltender coach who knows how to work with his athletes can be the difference in a team's being successful or not.

It is important for a goaltender coach to be extremely organized. You must have a large amount of structure and organizational skills when running drills on the ice. It is important to form routines in the way you perform and to be able to change the content of those routines based on what you feel the goaltenders need to work on most. Your approach and instruction must be consistent.

### Be Positive

As mentioned, coach from a "do," not a "don't, standpoint. Tell the goaltender what he needs to do, not what he shouldn't do. Always work from a positive. Although it can be frustrating if a goaltender isn't getting the idea of something you are trying to teach, it is imperative that you avoid demonstrating your frustration. More than likely, the goaltender is just as frustrated as you are, so you want to avoid creating a negative environment.

### Understand Your Goaltenders

It is important for the goalie coach to understand each of the goaltenders he is working with. Plan and come prepared to the rink. Consider the goalies you are working with, and come in with a strong lesson plan. Don't limit your goaltender based on what you think he can do. Get to work on fundamentals, and work to improve your goaltenders as much as possible. Always be available to correct mistakes made by the goaltender when performing the fundamentals.

People are different, and therefore you cannot treat every goaltender the same way. Understand your goalies' strengths and focus on the individual goaltender. One tactic that may work for one goalie may not work for another. For instance, a six-foot four-inch goaltender may be successful by always playing in his crease, whereas the five-foot six-inch goaltender may need to play a little farther out. Carey Price, Hendrik Lundqvist, and Jonathan Quick have similarities in their games, but they all do things a little differently.

### Push Your Goaltenders to Work Hard

There are times when it is necessary for you to be hard on your goaltender; however, sometimes the goalie doesn't respond the way you want. When this happens, approach him later and reiterate all the positive things he has done. The goal is always to create a positive learning experience. It is OK to push your goaltender hard physically. Not only do you want to create a technically efficient goaltender; you also want him to be able to continue to be at his best even when he's physically exhausted.

Eli discusses technique with a goaltender.

Eli Wilson works his goalies as hard as he can. If it is the day before a game, you can back off a little. It is better to go hard with quality rather than quantity. It is better to avoid extended ice times and five-day-a-week practices. Goaltending drills should be high tempo. The goaltending position is one of high intensity. Be hard on the shooters so they stay focused so drills are executed with as much detail and intensity as possible.

### Communicate Constructively and Concisely

Communication between a goaltender and his coach is important. The goalie coach needs to think about the best time to tell a goaltender something about his game and when it is best not to say anything. You don't want to be the coach who constantly tells the goalie "You're doing great." Constructive criticism such as "You're in good position to make the first save, but be sure to track the puck and follow the rebound" is far more effective. It is important to be straightforward yet positive with your goaltenders.

The goalie coach should be brief with his on-ice communication. The last thing anyone wants to see is the goalie coach going into long explanations with the goaltender during practice. All that does is use up valuable ice time. Instead, work with the goaltender off ice to design a series of words as quick reminders. For instance, if the goaltender is not watching the puck, rather than going into a long explanation about focusing on the puck, just say "eyes." The goaltender will know to keep his eyes on the puck. The goalie coach is not talking in code; he is just abbreviating what has been previously taught.

Eli giving brief instruction.

Overcoaching occurs when a goalie coach goes over to the goaltender after each shot in practice and points out things the goaltender needs to correct. Don't try to make everything perfect in practice. If you see the goaltender making glaring errors, focus on a couple of things during that ice time. It is always better to concentrate on a few tactics each practice with the goaltender. Let the goaltender face several shots before giving any pointers. This allows the goaltender to get into the flow of the practice without being overwhelmed with too many pointers from the goalie coach. Remember, sometimes less is more.

### Get to Know Your Goaltenders

Getting to know your goaltenders on a personal level is always a good way to build the relationship between the coach and the player. You should discuss other things besides goaltending with one another. Talk about other interests. What else does the goaltender do in life? Creating a personal bond between you and the goaltenders only enhances the probability for positive results.

### Be Open Minded

You must be ready to constantly adapt to changes in the game. Be innovative and don't be closed minded. Allow your goaltenders to be individuals. Not every goaltender is going to do things the same way. To put this concept in perspective, think about two people walking across a room. They are both trying to achieve the same thing, getting to the other side of the room. However, they may move differently from one another, they don't look the same, and their balance may be different; yet they both achieve the same result. The same thing applies to goaltending. Two goaltenders have the same goal, for instance, both are facing a shot from the slot and their intent is to make the initial save and cover the puck. Their methods to achieve this result may be slightly different from one another. One goaltender may play a little farther out of his crease, and the other may be taller and play back near the goal line; yet they both make the initial save and smother the rebound.

As a coach, you can't have the attitude that "everyone is doing it this way, so this is how I will teach it." That's not to say that there aren't some fundamentals to be followed, but remember that every person is different and it is up to you to bring out the best in each goaltender based on his strengths. It is important as a goalie coach to believe in your players and encourage them.

Also, when working with goaltenders, it is important to be in the present and teach the game as it is now. Referring to goaltenders from decades past and how they played the position is irrelevant and not relatable to the goaltender. Goaltending is constantly advancing. It is OK to respect the history of the game and refer to goalies from the recent past; however, try to keep everything in relation to the present day in terms of teaching.

### Act as a Liaison

You may be required to work as a liaison between the goaltender and the head coach. Remember, the head coach has a full slate of things to work on with his team and may not have the ability to focus on the goaltenders. Head coaches just want a goaltender who can stop the puck. Many head coaches don't talk to the goaltenders and leave that communication up to you. Some head coaches are close to their goaltenders, whereas others distance themselves. Both strategies have been effective at all levels. You must have an understanding as to what type of head coach you are working with and communicate accordingly.

### Teach Simply and Progressively

Goaltenders must learn in progression. For example, you may see goaltenders working on inside-edge pushes before they work on proper T-pushes and butterfly slides. If the position is not taught in a specific order, then you end up with goalies with diverse levels of balance and consistency. This book, for example, progresses through stance to save execution and on to postsave recoveries and puck handling. You don't want to teach your goaltender how to follow a rebound before showing him how to properly execute a save.

We recommend that you start every goalie session with basic movement drills that relate to the day's lesson plan. When it comes to skating, goaltenders should work on crease movement drills and navigating efficiently in the net. They are good for conditioning, balance movement, and structure. The same holds true for camps and private sessions. Also, as a side note about safety, when starting your skating drills, do not leave pucks lying around because they pose a danger for all players on the ice. Pucks can create a tripping hazard with serious consequences.

Keep your drills clean and simple, and don't overcomplicate them with too many things happening at one time. Be direct and to the point with smooth, clean drills and clear direction. For example, if you want your goaltender to make a save, direct the puck into the corner, and follow the rebound while tracking opposition players, your instruction should be as follows: "Push out, stop hard, make the save, and follow the rebound; get on your post and apply soft focus." These simple instructions inform the goaltender of everything he needs to know to execute the drill.

Gray areas can be incorporated into the drill. Gray areas are components that are added to a drill to create unpredictability. Using the example above, after the goaltender directs the puck into the corner, you could have a player pass the puck out front to another skater for a second shot on goal. The goaltender does not know where the player in front will shoot, and he will be forced to use his instincts to read the play and react. Don't create cookie-cutter goaltenders. Incorporate structure, but make it so your goaltender is adaptable to different situations. Keep the drills simple. Run drills with discipline. Make sure your shooters are positioned properly and taking the types of shots you require of them. If you incorporate structure into your drills, both the goaltender and the shooters will benefit.

Note that most goalie coaches not only work with goaltenders on a team but also train goalies in camps. There is a big difference between instructing goaltenders in a camp atmosphere and working with two goaltenders on a team. In a camp the coaches work with multiple goalies at once with access to shooters as needed. They usually have a limited number of days to work with the goaltenders, so they tend to throw a lot at them in a short time. On a team, the goalie coach works with two goaltenders daily with the opportunity to improve them over a longer period. It is important to recognize the differences and what it is you are trying to accomplish with your goaltenders from day to day.

### Teach Team Concepts

In a team environment, the coach may run a series of drills that are meant for the skaters and not the goaltenders. The goaltender needs to continue to compete without getting frustrated or losing confidence because goals are being scored. Remember that the players are working on their game as well. Drills where the shooters are constantly in a scoring position are unrealistic for the goaltender if they are in rapid succession, but he must power through it for the betterment of the team. You should not judge your goaltenders based on such a practice where shooters are constantly in optimal scoring position. That many scoring opportunities in succession would normally not happen in a game. It is up to you to make sure the goaltender maintains his confidence.

In a team setting, it is important that you and your two goaltenders form a small family unit. A backup goaltender should play his role and wait for his chance to play. You may have different expectations of your starter and the backup, but you must stay in it together as a team. Use the starter as a role model for the backup to aspire to. It is part of your responsibility to manage both goaltenders on the team and keep them motivated. If you have a goaltender who is upset about playing time, motivate him to work harder because that will increase his odds of playing as opposed to sulking. Expectations of the backup goaltender are discussed in more detail later in this chapter.

### Work Through Slumps

All goaltenders go through periods when things just aren't coming together, known as a slump. How the goaltender overcomes a slump depends heavily on his character. You also play an important role during these times. It is not a good idea for you to spoon-feed a goalie with compliments (e.g., it's not your fault) as he struggles through a slump. It is better to let the goaltender get stronger and work his way through the tough times. Remain positive with your goaltender, but reiterate that hard work is the answer to working through the slump. Goaltenders who don't believe hard work is the answer tend to have long slumps. They are inclined to overthink everything that has gone wrong, and the problems just continue to compound.

A goaltender must fight through adversity. It is important that the goaltender approach the next game with an "I'm going to win this" as opposed to an "I hope I don't lose again" attitude. He must learn not to get too high during the good times and not too low when facing adversity. You play a key role in helping the goaltender stay grounded and consistent.

### Use Video Analysis

It is great to use video to analyze goaltenders and study what their tendencies are. It is beneficial for both the goaltender and you; however, there is a balance. On the one hand, you want to show the goaltender enough video to illustrate things that you want him to improve on, but you don't want to inundate him with too much video analysis and too many ideas on how to fix his game. Always show one or two things, and then work on those. Too much video can become a detriment. Some goalie coaches prefer reviewing video with their goaltenders on the ice during practice. It is better to analyze video with the goaltender off the ice and use the on-ice time more effectively working on error correction. There are a couple of exceptional video analysis programs that allow you to monitor your goaltender's progression on a game-to-game basis over the course of a season.

Video analysis on the ice.

### *Cooperate With Other Coaches*

Many goaltenders go to private training sessions and camps throughout the season and off-season. This can create a challenging situation for a team's goalie coach. The coach whom the goaltender trains with outside of the team may have conflicting views with you. It can be detrimental to a goaltender's development if one coach is talking negatively about another through the goaltender to make himself look better. It is much like the "divorced parents' syndrome" whereby each parent talks poorly about the other to the kids. All the disparaging remarks do is bring negative energy to the teaching process. Bashing other coaches just creates confusion for goaltenders. It is far more productive for you to say, "Those are valid tactics that you have been shown, but here is why I want you to do it this way." That way the goaltender can remain confident in both his goalie coaches.

# THE HEAD COACH

As stated earlier, some head coaches build relationships with their goaltenders, whereas others communicate to their goaltenders through the goalie coach. Eli Wilson believes that a positive relationship between the goaltenders and all the coaches on the team will result in better production from the goaltenders. Whichever style the head coach believes in, the following principles should apply.

### Be Positive With Your Goaltenders

It is essential that you stay positive with the goaltenders. Give the goaltenders some leeway to work through challenging times. It is never a good idea to keep your goaltenders on a short string. If the goalie believes he will be pulled after every bad goal, then his focus becomes attached to worrying more about not getting scored on than stopping pucks. There is a big difference in the mindset between the two (see chapter 8). If your goaltender struggles early in the game, it is never a bad idea to pull him for a short time and then put him back in the net. This allows the goaltender to regain his composure while letting him know that you still have faith in him to win the game.

If you have concerns about your goaltender, you should express those thoughts to the goalie coach, who in turn can relate them to the goaltender. This allows the goalie coach time to prepare his drills with the goaltender for the next practice. The environment that you as head coach need to create in the dressing room is one of continuous improvement. Things are not always going to go as planned, and it is important that you understand that and work to improve not only the goaltenders but all the players on the team. Threatening the goaltender or directly blaming him for certain goals allowed will only heighten the goaltender's anxiety level and surely lead to even worse results. If you want to get the best production out of your goaltenders, be patient and stay positive.

### Confer With Goalie Coach When Choosing Starting Goalie

Decide with your goalie coach who is going to get what starts. Involve your goalie coach in that decision-making process because he is the one working with the goaltenders daily and he should have a better feel for each goaltender's current mindset.

### Give Starting Goalie Time to Prepare

It is not a good idea to wait until game time to let a goalie know that he is starting. Goalies should be made aware about a day before the game. Similarly, there is no advantage to telling a goalie too far in advance that he is playing. Twenty-four hours is ideal. In a tournament situation where you may have two games in one day, let the goalies know who will be starting as soon as possible following the end of the first game. The backup goaltender must be ready to go if called upon. However, understand that the pregame preparation as a backup is different from that of the starter.

### Incorporate Goaltenders Into Team Practices

Most of a team practice should be designed for the skaters. You need to run your team through such things as breakout drills, penalty killing, power plays, and defensive zone coverage. However, goaltenders need time in practice to work on their game. The concept that a goalie will improve because he will see a lot of shots in a practice is not altogether true. As a head coach, you can design your drills to incorporate the goaltenders into more realistic gamelike scenarios. There is no such thing as a drill that is "for the goalies only" when shooters are involved. If you make drills competitive for both the goaltenders and the shooters, it helps to build camaraderie on the team. Be open minded to having certain handed shooters in positions to make the drill most effective; don't just line shooters up indiscriminately. Drills should be set up to give both the goaltenders and the shooters optimal opportunity to improve.

If you run a drill that is more goaltender specific, you can add a component to it that allows the shooter to improve his game at the same time, such as incorporating a second shot whereby the shooter tries to score. That way the shooter stays fully engaged in the drills. Make your drills shot specific. If you want a goaltender to recover to his blocker side, make sure the shooter puts the puck to that side. You don't want the skater arbitrarily picking a side to shoot and then expect the goaltender to recover to a predetermined side. However, as previously mentioned, you can make the second shot a "shoot-to-score" scenario, allowing the shooter some freedom in where he wants to direct the shot.

If you feel that an ice session has lost intensity, you may choose to have the whole team perform wind sprints at the end of practice. Wind sprints occur when the team skates the length of the ice and back numerous times. If you skate the team as a group, then the goaltenders must join in. If the goaltenders do not participate, then a division is created between the goaltenders and the rest of the team.

Also, remember to give your team days off. Rest is important because it allows players to refocus and overcome any small, nagging injuries.

### *Learn How to Compromise*

It is always a balancing act for head coaches when it comes to incorporating goaltender training into team practices. The following suggestions help to alleviate this issue. You can allow 15 minutes at the start of each practice for the goalie coach to work with the goalies. Once the time is up, the goaltenders join the rest of the team for the duration of the practice. Another option is if there are multiple practices each week, you can take one of those ice times and hold a skills session with your skaters on three-quarters of the ice while the goalie coach works with the goalies at the other end. Shooters can come in and out as needed to assist the goalie coach. However you decide to structure your practices, it is important to find a balance whereby the goaltender is getting the training he requires while also being available to help the rest of his team improve. This is discussed in more detail in the next section of this chapter.

# THE GOALTENDER

Goaltending is an all-consuming position in the game of hockey. As the last line of defense, you are constantly under pressure to perform and provide your team the best chance to win. It is easy to let the pressure of the position eat you up. Eli Wilson believes in the importance of goaltenders' maintaining a work/life balance. The following are some tools you can use to help maintain your equilibrium throughout a long season.

### Understand Your Responsibilities

You have many responsibilities to your teammates, coaches, and team personnel. As a goaltender, you are different from the other players on your team because you play an individual position in a team setting. At the same time, you should be there for your team. Your responsibility is to be the best goaltender you can be in both practices and games.

Goaltenders often feel that they are nothing more than targets in many team practices. This is not the attitude you want to have. Instead, be competitive in all drills, but understand that if there is a rapid succession of skaters who shoot from a high scoring percentage area, then you are going to give up a lot of goals. Don't get frustrated or lose confidence; just keep competing. Sometimes, you must "suck one up" for the team.

### Respect the Game

Always respect the game, the position, and your coach. Do the things that the coach asks of you and always be the best you can be. Understand that some drills are not designed for the goaltender. Don't pout about it, and don't break your stick over the net in frustration.

Respect teammates, parents, trainers, and everyone at the rink. Your parents don't have to pay for your hockey or send you to goalie schools, so respect the privilege you have been afforded to play the game of hockey.

### Maximize Your Practice Time

If a practice consists of mostly odd-man rush drills, it is important for you to compete on every repetition and pay attention to detail. By doing this, you involve yourself in the drill in a meaningful way and eliminate yourself from being a target. You can study the creativity of the players and control your depth. Am I challenging or not? Am I holding my position? Try to play through these sorts of drills as if you were in a game.

You don't want to go on the ice "as hard as you can" with no purpose or thought behind what you are trying to accomplish. It is important to talk with the goalie coach and think about things that will make you a better goaltender. Also, when working in practice, think about what the key points to the drill are. What do I need to focus on to be effective? Evaluate yourself, and if you find something is not working for you, discuss it with your goalie coach.

### Separate Home Life and Hockey

When you are at home, live your family life. Don't bring the games home with you. Whether you played a good game or not, let it go and focus on the people around you. Don't drag your goaltending into your family life and vice versa. Be in the moment of everything you do in your life. Keep your goaltending and your home life separate because the position alone takes an immense amount of focus to be successful.

### Maintain Confidence

If you are going through a tough period on the ice, try to make yourself feel good. Think about good things in your life. Being able to replace negative thoughts with positive thoughts will help you maintain your confidence and give you a better chance at turning your game around. Have interests and hobbies outside the game. It is beneficial to be involved in other activities besides goaltending; it's important to have distractions from the game.

### Stay Present in Your Thoughts

Don't think about the past, and don't think too far into the future. What happens if we lose? What happens if they score? Avoiding these thoughts is one of the hardest things for goaltenders to do. Just focus on what is happening on the ice in front of you right then.

It is always a good idea to get yourself mentally prepared for a game, but don't overthink it too far in advance. Perform some visualization the night before and then let it go. When you get to the rink, start warming up your body and then begin to think about the game.

### Document Your Progress

Keep a journal on your progression throughout the season. When things are going well, write down how you feel and all the positives associated with that feeling. When things are not as good, you can reflect back on how you felt when things were going well and aim to reclaim those feelings again. How did I feel when things were good?

### Be Coachable

Coachability means that the goaltender does what the coach asks him to do. Be open minded with your coaches. If your goalie coach gives you a suggestion for improvement, don't answer with a "Yeah but." The goalie coach is making suggestions for you to improve; your success is his success. If you want to continue doing exactly what you have always done, you won't improve. Try to get on the same page as your goalie coach. It is never a bad idea to watch other goalies to see what you can learn from them.

At some time in their careers, all goaltenders will experience the long skate from the net to the bench when being pulled from a game. Although it can be a deflating experience, the key is not to sulk. Don't smash your stick over your net or at the bench because it is far more effective to stay calm and regroup. You never know whether the coach will ask you to go back into the game. Don't be too hard on yourself because there could be a variety of reasons why the coach has decided to make a goaltending change.

### Be a Leader

Be dedicated to the team and have a strong work ethic. Make sure you are never the last player on the ice for team practices. Never fear the competition, whether it be the other goaltender on your team or any team in your league. There are some goaltenders who fear playing in a deciding playoff game or overtime. The goaltender who can control his nerves has an advantage over the goalie who can't. Always be the goaltender who embraces the competition and opportunity to win the big game. Great goaltenders lead their teams both on and off the ice with the intention of winning a championship.

### Communicate Effectively With the Head Coach

It can be a frustrating experience to compete in a practice where the whole ice time is dedicated to odd-man rushes and flow drills. Goaltenders get peppered with many shots in those types of practices and will more than likely be scored on a lot. Instead of cornering the head coach to make suggestions on how he should change drills to accommodate you as a goaltender, you should simply tell him that you are struggling with a certain component of your game and would like to work with the goalie coach on it a little more next practice. The message you are sending to the head coach is that you are looking for ways to improve yourself. A coach will be receptive to that approach.

We talked earlier about compromise between the head coach and the goaltender. If you are getting 15 to 20 minutes at the start of practice to work on your skills, then you need to work hard in every drill and be there for your team for the remainder of the practice.

On a related note, many coaches are intense and can appear to be hard on their goaltenders. Keep in mind that the coach wants you to be successful and has the best interest of the team at heart. If your head coach puts pressure on you, don't take it in a negative light. Instead, use it as a training ground for learning how to deal with people. As you progress through the ranks of hockey, you may find that some coaches are extremely hard on their goaltenders, so you need to prepare yourself for that. Some of the negativity may come from the head coach's lack of knowledge regarding the difficulty in playing the position. The physical and mental demands on goaltenders are immense. Learn how to adapt to the coach and don't let it affect your play. A negative coach doesn't affect you in a physical sense, so it is up to you to not let it affect you emotionally. Continue to work hard and prove to your coach that you can get the job done.

# THE BACKUP GOALTENDER

The head coach should stipulate early in the season who the starter and the backup are. As the backup, you need to work hard in practice to take some of the load off the starter. Your goal should be to work as hard as possible with the intent of taking the starter's job at some point. Moping or feeling sorry for yourself won't cut it in a team environment. You need to be a good teammate to the starting goaltender. There needs to be a good relationship between the two of you whereby you push each other to get better. Although battling for the starting job creates competition, you don't want to create a negative environment. If you and the starting goaltender don't get along, it will create a rift in the dressing room. Both of you will have friends on the team, and you will start to see a divide among players, with some supporting the starter and others supporting you. Divisions in the dressing room are a surefire way for a team to fail.

When you are on the bench as a backup, you still need to be mentally dialed into the game. Lots of players sit on the bench and zone out or question themselves as to why they aren't playing. Suddenly, the starting goaltender is out of the game, and the backup is called in but is not prepared to play. As a backup goaltender, you must be engaged and watch the game, look for tendencies of opposing players, watch the power play, and study the other team.

Whether you are a head coach, a goalie coach, or a goaltender, effective communication is key in order to maintain a positive team environment. Head coaches must decide if they are going to deal directly with their goaltenders or through the goalie coach. Once the decision is made, it is imperative that the coach maintain consistent lines of communication. Goalie coaches must always come to the rink prepared with a practice plan that will work on areas where the goaltender needs the most improvement. Goaltenders need to come to the rink each day prepared to work hard and help their teammates improve during practices. It is a delicate balance to keep starting goaltenders, backup goaltenders, teammates, and coaches on the same page throughout the long hockey season, but if everybody works together in a positive environment the team's chances for success increase dramatically.

# How Much Is Too Much?

If a player shows a desire to engage in spring and summer hockey, let him play. It is up to the individual. If he wants to get away from hockey and play baseball or other sports, then let him experience those. If a goaltender wants to play on two spring hockey clubs at the end of his winter team's season and the parents can afford it, then let him do it. It all comes down to the desires of the player. If a goaltender wants to be at the rink more than anything else, then playing in the spring will not burn him out. There is a limit, however, and all players do need time away from the rink and game. The amount of required time off is dependent on an individual's needs and desires.

Don't feel that an athlete needs to play a variety of sports to improve at his primary sport? Tiger Woods focused on golf only and was one of the most dominant athletes of his generation. If Woods had played baseball, would it have made him a better golfer? Probably not. NHL superstars Connor McDavid and Austin Mathews both played hockey in the summer. They may have played other sports recreationally but nothing competitive. They focused on hockey. That's not to say that parents should run out and sign their kids up for endless amounts of spring and summer hockey. It all comes down to a person's enjoyment of living. If an athlete wants to play other sports, don't stop him, but if he wants to focus on his number one sport, there is nothing wrong with that either.

Many off-ice training programs are designed to work muscles that you don't use for your primary sport. A properly designed off-ice program combined with on-ice training will give your muscles the same variety of use as playing a multitude of sports will. Contrary to public opinion, playing multiple sports is a personal choice. There is no right or wrong.

# About the Authors

Eli Wilson has established himself as one of the premier goaltending coaches in the world. He has worked with dozens of goaltenders in the National Hockey League (NHL), including Carey Price, Ray Emery, Tim Thomas, Tuukka Rask, Brian Elliott, Jason LaBarbera, and Devan Dubnyk.

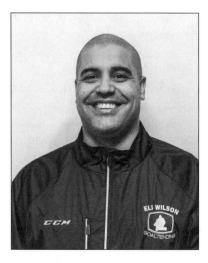

Under his tutelage, Eli's camps have produced more than 50 NHL draft picks, over 60 Division I or Canadian University goaltenders, and more than 200 players drafted by Major Junior teams. His goaltenders have gone on to win numerous prestigious awards and championships: Stanley Cups, Conn Smythe Trophies, Venzina Trophies, World Junior Gold Medals, American Hockey League (AHL) championships, AHL Playoff MVPs, WHL Goaltender of the Year, Ontario Hockey League (OHL) Goaltender of the Year, and Canadian Hockey League (CHL) Goaltender of the Year.

In 2004, Eli founded World Pro Goaltending and was instrumental in developing it into one of the largest goaltending schools and training facilities in Canada. When he departed from the company in 2009, World Pro Goaltending was performing more than 5,000 one-on-one training sessions annually, along with numerous camps, including the world-renowned Elite Prospects and Professional (NHL) camps.

In 2004, Eli was also named to Hockey Canada's goaltending consultant group, along with Francois Allaire and Sean Burke. Since 2004, he has consulted with Creative Artists Agency (CAA) Sports during their summer development camps for top young prospects in Los Angeles, California. From 2003-2007, Eli served as the goaltending coach of the Medicine Hat Tigers of the Western Hockey League. During the 2004 and 2007 Championship seasons, goaltenders Kevin Nastiuk and Matt Keetley were named WHL playoff MVPs respectively. In 2007, Eli traveled to South Korea to work with the Kangwon Land Ice Hockey team and other young goaltenders in the country.

From 2007 through 2010, Eli was the goaltending coach for the Ottawa Senators, where he was responsible for the Ottawa Senators goaltenders as well as for the goalies playing for their AHL affiliate, the Binghamton Senators. In February 2011, Eli was hired by the Anaheim Ducks to work as the goaltending consultant for their affiliate, the Syracuse Crunch.

In 2010, Eli established Eli Wilson Goaltending. Today, Eli Wilson Goaltending is a world leader in goaltending development. Eli runs goaltending camps, clinics, and consults worldwide. In 2016, Eli introduced a number of specialty camps, including the popular 24/7, where goaltenders actually live and train with Eli over a three-day weekend. He has skill-specific camps, including puck-handling camps and tactical and situational camps,  and in 2017 he started running camps that bring  together top prospect forwards and goaltenders to create a high-intensity training environment. A main staple of Eli's year-round training is advanced video technology, whereby he and his staff can analyze video remotely to further goaltending development.

Brian van Vliet has a diverse sporting background. He played competitive soccer for six years and competed in numerous bodybuilding competitions, including the prestigious 1993 Canadian Bodybuilding Championships in Montreal, Quebec. Having studied the position of goaltending for many years, Brian was a member of the board of directors for a local hockey association and served as the goalie coordinator for three years. He was responsible for the evaluation and placement of over 70 goaltenders annually.

Brian was an associate writer of Eli Wilson's "In the Crease" column for the Alberta edition of Hockey Now magazine and later went on to author his own monthly opinion piece for the same publication. His experience as a continuous improvement professional in the oil and gas industry gives him a unique and analytical approach to the game of hockey. Having attained a business management degree from Davenport University, Brian is currently the vice president of business operations for Eli Wilson Goaltending and also works as a real estate agent in Calgary.